The Campus Life Guide to _____
━━━━━━━━━━━━━ **Surviving High School**

THE CAMPUS LIFE GUIDE TO

Surviving High School

Edited by Verne Becker

ZONDERVAN PUBLISHING HOUSE
OF THE ZONDERVAN CORPORATION
GRAND RAPIDS, MICHIGAN 49506

CAMPUS LIFE BOOKS
A DIVISION OF YOUTH FOR CHRIST
WHEATON, ILLINOIS 60187

Zondervan/Campus Life Books are published by
Zondervan Publishing House,
1415 Lake Drive, S.E.,
Grand Rapids, Michigan 49506

The Campus Life Guide to Surviving High School
© 1984 by Verne Becker

Library of Congress Cataloging in Publication Data

Main entry under title:

The Campus life guide to surviving high school.

Summary: A guide to coping with the conflicts and changes of the
high school years, including feelings, family relationships, and one's own
body. Uses firsthand stories of people who have found God helpful.
    1. High school students—Conduct of life—Addresses, essays,
lectures.   2. High school students—Religious life—Addresses,
essays, lectures.   [1. Conduct of life—Addresses, essays, lectures.
2. Christian life—Addresses, essays, lectures]   I. Becker, Verne.
II. Campus life.   III. Title: Surviving high school.
BJ1661.C16   1984   158'.088055   84-19654
ISBN 0-310-47141-9

Designed by Ann Cherryman

Printed in the United States of America

84 85 86 87 88 89 90 91 / 10 9 8 7 6 5 4 3 2 1

CONTENTS

INTRODUCTION

It's the first day of ~~high~~ school. You step off the school bus, unmarked spiral notebooks in hand, and merge into the mass of students making their way to the main door. As the crowd files into the freshly waxed, locker-lined hallways, you notice that the school seems larger and more sophisticated than your junior high did. And the people seem much older than you. Just last year you stood at the pinnacle of achievement of your previous school; you were the oldest and wisest—you had arrived. But now you wonder if you are anything but a twerpy, immature freshman.

For a few minutes, as you search for your locker, you're struck with a severe case of insecurity—maybe even downright fear. A hundred unarticulated questions flood your mind: *How will I fit in here? Will I be able to handle the work load? Who will I hang around with?* All the new faces, new clothes, new teachers, and new surroundings seem threatening. And during the first few weeks of school, you feel as if everyone else is gawking at you, laughing at your struggles in the same way Army personnel jeer at new recruits.

As if the stresses of ~~high~~ school aren't enough, you find that a whole new set of struggles awaits you when you get home from school each day. Your family relationships are changing. You're more aware of the way your parents get along—or don't get along. You probably clash with them more often over things like curfew, housecleaning or yard work, money, your bedroom, and your friends. And you're beginning to notice changes in yourself, too: slowly you're becoming aware of the way you feel about yourself, your body, your opinions, your emotions, your habits. These changes and new discoveries also bring stress.

With all these pressures closing in on you, you're bound to wonder sometimes whether you'll be able to cope. Or maybe you feel that way *all* the time. How can you handle all this change on so many fronts at once—in school, at home, and in yourself?

That's what this book is all about. It's a specially designed, practical guide for coping with the conflicts and changes you're facing right now. Think of it as a survival guide for your high-school years, a travel guide for the journey ahead.

You'll find a twofold approach for dealing with problems in this book. Each section opens with some broad advice, given by someone who has stood back and gained a little perspective. That general advice is followed by stories from people who have dealt with these problems firsthand. You'll hear not only strategic advice but the voice of experience as well.

As you read through this survival guide, and as you tackle some of the problems that lie ahead, I hope you'll discover two things: that ultimately what matters is not the problem, but how you deal with it, and that God wants to be a part of the process.

—Verne Becker

The Campus Life Guide to _____
_____ **Surviving High School**

Photo by Jean-Claude Lejeune

SECTION 1

FEELINGS

FEELINGS

Verne Becker

Once after a party someone threw an egg at me. It stung my right shoulder and splattered yellow-and-clear slime and broken shell bits all over my jacket.

Instantly infuriated, I wheeled around and yelled, "OK, who threw that egg? It's not funny!" When I saw that my brother Brad had thrown it, my anger boiled all the more, but for some reason I couldn't say anything to him. I think I feared that if I said even one word, I'd lose all control of myself. Instead, I defiantly climbed into the car beside my girlfriend and slammed the door.

There I sat, shaking in the front seat, my arms tightly crossed, fists clenched, and knuckles white, as if I could somehow physically restrain my anger. *I'm not going to let this get to me,* I kept telling myself.

My girlfriend didn't know what to do. "Verne, are you OK?" she said, bewildered. "I've never *seen* you like this before."

Neither had I. I had every right to be angry with Brad for pelting me with that egg, but the intensity of my feelings took me by surprise. As I sat there fuming in the front seat, I felt a strange compulsion to put a lid on my anger. I even tried to deny altogether that I was angry. I was faced with a dilemma: I couldn't bottle my feelings inside, yet I was also afraid to let them out.

As a college freshman, no matter how informal the situation, I always got nervous when I picked up the phone to ask out a girl.

"Uh, hello Barb—this is Verne. Uh, I was thinking of seeing the movie on campus tonight, and wondered if you'd like to go too."

"No, I don't think so," she said almost immediately. Her voice, though pleasant, had a note of finality that hurt a little.

Hoping to preserve my pride, I said, "Oh, that's too bad. You got a lot of studying to do tonight?"

"No, not really," Barb said, still offering no further explanation.

By now I didn't just hurt a little—I felt totally rejected and finished the conversation on a friendly note. That evening I went to the movie with a few guys from my floor, and even joked with them about my phone call. But it still hurt inside.

Maybe I was overly sensitive. Maybe she did have personal plans that she simply didn't want to tell me about. But the hurt stayed with me, and several weeks passed before I could muster the courage to ask someone out again.

Alan Alda once said that when he produced an episode of "M*A*S*H" he wanted the viewer to both laugh and cry within that half hour. With me, he often succeeds, even on the reruns. Between "M*A*S*H" and "Little House on the Prairie," I end up in tears almost every week. I guess I just identify with the joys and sorrows of the M*A*S*H characters and the Ingalls family. Sometimes an emotional scene will take place, and I'll stop and ask myself, "Why did I need to hide the fact that I am moved by this story? Am I embarrassed that it affected me this way?"

As I reflect on these experiences and as I compare stories with others, I realize that I'm not alone in my feelings. At various times all of us experience anger, hurt, rejection, joy, sadness, and a number of other emotions. Sometimes we're not really aware of them; they just simmer under the surface of our psyche, ready to erupt before we even know what happened.

Feelings seem so unpredictable, intense, even contradictory at times—what are we to make of them? Do we always have to be at their mercy and have to put up with them, or is there a way to understand our feelings and learn from them?

Road Signs

In recent years I've come to see that my feelings are a lot like road signs: they alert me to what's coming ahead. Signs may signal a rough road, construction, or a slippery surface, or they may give directions or distances that I should keep in mind as I travel.

I'm reminded of this nearly every time I drive west on Interstate 80 toward Chicago. I know the roads quite well, and pay hardly any attention to the traffic and the maze of highways weaving in and out of each other. But inevitably I forget about the onslaught of signs that occurs near the end of the Indiana Toll Road. They appear on my right, on my left, overhead, all at the same time. "Chicago," they all say, but they point in different directions. I know in my mind which road to take, but when I see all those signs at once my brain short-circuits.

Usually my reflexes respond quickly enough that I can jerk the steering wheel in the right direction at the last moment. But on several occasions I have simply forgotten to make a choice before taking the wrong exit. When I realize what I've done, I slam the steering wheel with my fist, scolding myself for not noticing the signs earlier. Then, of course, I have to drive another five or ten minutes until I can make a loop back to the proper exit. Even when I think I know the way to go, I still need to watch the signs so I can turn at the right times.

Cruising down I-80, the signs don't decide anything for me; I must decide for myself whether to exit at Route 53 or 83. But the signs give me vital information. I can't ignore them if I'm ever to arrive at my destination.

Our feelings operate in a similar way. They give us information that we can use to relate to other people, understand ourselves and our needs, and make decisions. For example, I'm sure that Brad intended no harm when he hit me with the egg, but my anger informed me that I was feeling mistreated. Or when Barb said no to my movie invitation, my feelings of hurt and rejection indicated the state of my self-image, which was very low at the time.

Like road signs, feelings don't carry any moral value; they aren't right or wrong in themselves. Neither do they make

The Campus Life Guide

any decisions for us; it is our *responses* to them that can be wrong. Yet real feelings are only pieces of information that rise to the surface as we encounter various people and situations. Our responsibility is to be aware of these feelings and learn to interpret the messages they are giving us. Only then can we make decisions and respond appropriately to the actions or words of other people.

Of course, it can be dangerous to base all of our actions and decisions solely on feelings, just as it can mean trouble to look only at road signs and never consult a map. But more often than not, we probably miss the important messages our feelings are sending us.

The Stuff of Life

While feelings may confuse and frustrate us at times, they are important for several reasons: First, life is full of feelings and we can't deny that. They are inescapable. Think about the past year—even your entire life. Think about the best times you had and the worst times: think how you felt at those times. Recall a time when your parents punished you; when you made (or failed to make) the cheerlead-

ing squad; when you first fell in love; when you learned that someone had spread a false rumor about you. All the pleasures and pains you've experienced throughout your life involve your emotions.

Second, feelings and how we show them influence the quality of our friendships. Think about your relationships with people and about which ones are the most meaningful. They are probably the ones in which you and the other person are able to share your feelings. Most of us have one or two friends we relate to at that deepest feeling level.

But if you have trouble making close friendships, it's probably because the other person or both of you haven't been able to share at the feeling level. The way to know somebody deeply is to find out how they feel about things. And for other people to know you, they have to see how you feel also. In his book *Why Am I Afraid To Tell You Who I Am?* author John Powell says, "To tell you about my thoughts is to locate myself in a category. To tell you about my feelings is to tell you about me."

A third reason feelings are so important is that as we share them with other people, we come to know ourselves better.

"I can only know as much of myself as I have the courage to confide in you," Powell continues. As we allow our feelings to rise to the surface so we can identify them, he explains, we discover patterns in our emotional reactions that tell us a great deal about who we are. And it is only when we know ourselves that we can begin to change the things we don't like about ourselves and our relationships. Listening to our feelings is the key to making this happen.

Feelings are important because we experience them all the time, because they are essential if we want to form close relationships, and because they help us to know ourselves so that we can grow.

But then, why do our feelings confuse, frustrate or frighten us so often? Why are they so strong and unpredictable? Why do they only seem to make matters worse rather than better? The answer is that most of us haven't learned how to listen to our feelings and to express them constructively. It is through this process of identifying and expressing our feelings appropriately that we learn and grow. But for many people this process doesn't happen naturally. Expressing feelings is something

we need to learn and to exercise over and over, like playing the piano or learning to speak French. So where do we start? Let's look at a possible situation in your home, where you are the main character, and see what your emotional response could be.

Healthy/Unhealthy

You're sitting around the dinner table with the rest of your family talking about school assignments for the week, work that needs to be done around the house, and what your weekend plans are. Before long you find yourself disagreeing with your parents on several points. You begin to feel hot, your neck and shoulder muscles tighten, and the argument is about to begin.

Now comes the moment of truth; from here the conversation—and your *self*—can go one or two ways: one that is destructive for family relationships or one that helps everyone. Let's check out some of the responses that are common to all of us.

Deny your feelings. If someone points at the steam coming out of your ears, just say, "I'm *not* angry"—as loudly as you need to say it to convince everyone. Try to tell yourself that it's just a difference of opinion. Ignore any churning that may be taking place in the pit of your stomach. If you need to, get up from the table and leave with a parting statement such as "Fine—do whatever you want. I shouldn't have brought up the subject."

Hide your feelings. Don't let on that something's bothering you. Instead, focus on the argument, and do your best to be rational and win it. Do everything you can to "stay on top of things." If you need to make a joke out of the situation to ease the tension (and sidestep the truth), do so. A sarcastic remark with a double meaning may help. Or you can always resort to the silent treatment.

Do whatever your feelings tell you. If you feel like belting someone, go ahead—he probably deserves it anyway. After all, look at what he did to you. If you prefer the verbal attack, be sure it's clear that the other person is wrong and that the situation is his fault.

All of these approaches to resolving conflicts are based on your feelings, and result in complicating matters. Consequently, it is not enough to merely be aware of your feelings; something else must be applied. In his book *Why Am I Afraid To Tell You Who I Am?* John Powell offers some helpful steps for dealing constructively with your feelings. Picture yourself back at the dining-room table and consider this approach.

Listen to your feeling. "Turn your mind briefly away from the argument and pay direct attention to your emotional reaction. Ask yourself: What am I feeling?"

Admit the feeling to yourself. "Take a good look, so you can identify it. Estimate, too, how strong it is. It is anger, e.g., and it is pretty high voltage, too."

Find out what's behind your feeling. "If you really want to find out a lot about yourself, ask your anger how it got there and where it came from. Trace the origin of your emotion." For example, even though your first reaction was anger, you may begin to realize underneath that you've always felt inferior around your parents or that you've never been able to live up to their standards. It's very common for anger to mask other deeper feelings of hurt, rejection, or failure. These are the feelings that can tell you the most about yourself. But you may not discover them unless you take time to look.

Report your feeling. "Just the facts now. No interpretations or judgments. 'Let's cool it for a minute. I'm getting too worked up, and I'm starting to say things I don't mean.' It is very important not to accuse or judge in this report. Do not tell him that it is his fault that you got so angry. . . . Don't blame him even to yourself."

Integrate your feeling. "Having listened to your emotion, and having questioned it and reported it, now let your mind judge what is the right thing to do." Maybe you need to say, "Could we try it one more time? I think I've been too defensive to listen to you." Or maybe you need to drop the subject for some time in order for you to explore why your feelings are so strong.

Powell's books are helpful when it comes to feelings and relationships—well worth a closer look. But in this chapter and in those that follow, you'll discover a healthy approach to dealing with your feelings. You'll see that to deny or cover them up is essentially an act of dishonesty—to others and to yourself.

No matter how hard we may try, we cannot hide our feelings completely. We all give out or spill these emotions in one way or another. Some of us who seem very calm and collected may explode in violent rages on occasion. Others of us may slam doors, squeal tires, compete viciously in sports, overeat, or starve. Still others may get headaches, insomnia, stomach disorders, skin rashes or muscle spasms. Researchers have proved that all of these "behaviors" can stem from trying to deny feelings that lie beneath the surface. Their conclusion? Feelings need to be identified and expressed. The trick is learning to listen to what those feelings are saying to you and then to express them in a truthful, non-accusatory way.

As I struggle with my own personal problems and relationships, feelings of one sort or another rise up within me nearly every day. Sometimes they're vague and I can't seem to identify them. They gnaw away at me for days, sometimes weeks. But I've found that when I've listened to my feelings, identified them, reported and integrated them, my problems suddenly seem more manageable and not nearly as oppressive as before. I also sense that my life is going in the direction I want it to go, and, I believe, the way God wants it to go. Like road signs, our feelings can tell us a lot, if we'll only look at them.

COVER-UP

S. Rickly Christian

It was easy to feel good about Sharon, because all we ever did together was go to the movies, concerts, and football games. We scrambled from one date to another, too busy to spend much time talking or listening to each other about deeper things. So when our dating relationship fizzled after a few months, I didn't feel I had ever really known her.

She seemed like a pretty normal sixteen-year-old at the time. Her parents, brother, and sister also seemed fairly normal—she had no obvious cause for emotional upheaval. Sharon was a Christian and was popular in the church's youth group and in Campus Life meetings at school.

Shortly after we broke up she began dating somebody else. That romance soured before long, and she started going out with another guy. When that relationship crashed I was away at college.

About that time, a friend back home wrote to tell me Sharon had flipped and was in the hospital. She had been fooling with razor blades, testing how much she would bleed if she slashed herself. Her parents happened to find her in time and called an ambulance.

My mind fogged. I couldn't figure out why Sharon would do something that stupid. She had seemed to have everything under control—then this. I tried, but I couldn't comprehend the despair that finally prompted her to believe suicide was the answer.

That she was a Christian especially bothered me because, I reasoned, she had a power within greater than herself and should have been able to cope with any problem. It seemed that if Sharon really believed in God, I mean *really* believed, she shouldn't have cracked. Hers was a problem of too little faith, I concluded.

At the time, I was a new Christian and assumed the panacea for all problems was my self-righteous offering: "What you need is more faith." Other Christians I knew always seemed to be happy and controlled no matter what the occasion. If they scored

I got the impression it was important for Christians not to be overly emotional.

at the top of the class, they smiled. Their demeanor never seemed to change. So I got the impression it was important for Christians not to be overly emotional.

I learned to stifle deep personal feelings such as grief, anger, despair, bitterness or jealousy, because I felt "born-again believers" were supposed to have more control of themselves than your typical John Q. Public. I figured I could expect the average guy on campus to act in a "bizarre" manner because he is without God's control of his life, but Christians should be calm and always pleasant because God has given them a special ability to cope with life. And if you go around expressing negative emotions openly, well, it's obvious that you are not behaving like a mature Christian. You've lost control.

Several years have passed since I learned of Sharon's breakdown. With time I've come to feel differently about the incident and the extreme emotions that overwhelmed her. She bottled her feelings inside, perhaps believing it was wrong as a Christian to feel like she did about the seeming chaos in her life, and so

chose not to talk to her friends about her problems. Or maybe she did talk to them, and they said what I thought—that she wouldn't feel like she did if she had stronger faith. I wish I had known sooner that there are no easy answers when a person feels slam-dunked by emotions.

I recently received a late-night telephone call from California. A close friend of mine had just been operated on for cancer. The surgeon had cut away half the muscles in his neck, but even then couldn't unearth all the cancerous stringers that were rooted like crab grass throughout my friend's body. Barring a miracle, I was told, Mark would die within twelve months.

I didn't feel very spiritual at that point. Moments after I hung up, I burst into burning tears and slammed my fist against the wall. Over the years Mark and I had talked for long hours about goals and ambitions. I wanted to write; he wanted to practice law. I am now doing what I've always wanted, but Mark, in his final year of law school, might not live to see graduation day.

If I try to cover up . . . God knows I am just pretending. After all, he created me.

After crying for hours, I looked in the mirror. The reflection I saw would not fit the Marlboro Man image of masculinity. I saw bloodshot eyes, a tear-streaked face—a reflection of myself as I am, created by God not without feelings but with the capacity to be incredibly hurt and to express that inward pain.

When I received the phone call about Mark's surgery, tears were therapeutic for me. They allowed me to express my grief and deal with inner torment. But in many cases, crying only provides a partial release without solving the problem itself. A good cry may have been a good first step for Sharon, but she needed to talk about her feelings with somebody, whether a friend, parent, pastor, or counselor.

Sharon also needed to talk to God about her hurt. I've come to learn that he understands when others don't. His son spent thirty-three years on earth and daily had to deal with the passions and emotions that grip every human being. Jesus did not live a "greenhouse" kind of existence, safe and insulated from troubles. He felt the depths of rejection, loneliness, and despair. For example, when his good friend Lazarus died, Jesus wept. And then, the Bible notes, he prayed.

When I read such passages, I realize that if Jesus didn't have to cover up his feelings by flaunting an attitude of spiritual self-sufficiency, I shouldn't. Sometimes I don't feel able to cope. And if I try to cover up . . . and seem strong to others, God knows I am just pretending. After all, he created me.

Paul Tournier, the famous Swiss counselor, has written that "the act of confessing one's weakness is a stronger one than that of covering it up with noisy exhibitions of strength." The Apostle Paul must have been thinking something similar when he wrote, "When I recognize that I am weak, then I am strong because of my dependence on God."

SUMMER
SPIRIT

Ruth Senter

It was the last day of school before summer break. All winter long we had stood in chemistry class behind our test tubes and Bunsen burners and watched wistfully as Chickees Creek flowed through the clumps of pines, out past the rail fence toward the covered bridge and the foothills beyond.

Today we experienced our first taste of summer freedom, compliments of Mr. Wilkerson, who canceled fourth hour chemistry. "Sort of a vacation present to you all," he said. So we all went down to the creek to lie around, soak up some rays, and toss a Frisbee.

I remember Margaret that day too. When we finally convinced her the grass stains wouldn't ruin her white jeans, she came over and sat beside me. I skipped stones for awhile. She tried once or twice and then quit. "All those stones end up in the creek and the bank will erode away," she said.

And there were the dandelion chains we made into necklaces. Margaret finally picked a bunch of the yellow blossoms and started braiding while delivering a running commentary on the difficulty of getting dandelion color and smell out from under fingernails. I began to see the tips of my fingers turning a sick greenish yellow.

And funny that I hadn't noticed the mosquitoes until Margaret showed me the two big welts on her ankle. I started to itch. The grass began to prick me. Then Margaret said she was allergic to bee stings, and I began to worry about the bee buzzing around the honeysuckle behind us.

By the time fourth hour chemistry by the creek was over, I felt as if my spirits had been flattened by a steam-roller. I wondered if Margaret ever had a fun day in her whole life. I felt sad for her. But at the same time I wanted to shake her and say: *Margaret, can't you please tell me what you enjoy about spring and creeks and covered bridges? Let me know what you like about yourself, about me, about Mr. Wilkerson's chemistry class. Surely there's something positive somewhere. Your gloom rubs off on people. And they don't like it. Can't you do or say something to make my day more fun because I've been with you?*

*T*hen there was Ann, another classmate. During my winter quarter finals in college, she and I stayed up all night cramming for an 8:00 A.M. English exam. It didn't help that the cafeteria served oatmeal for breakfast that morning or that we had to trudge through one of the worst blizzards of the season to get to class. And to top it off, the test covered three chapters Ann and I hadn't even looked at. By the time the exam was over I was ready to swallow a couple aspirin and go to bed. There was nothing worth staying up for as far as I was concerned.

Ann should have felt worse. My problems didn't begin to compare with the load she was carrying. She hadn't heard from her boyfriend back home for three weeks. And the day before the exam she received news that her sister had given birth to a Mongoloid baby.

I waited for Ann in the coffee shop after the exam. She bounced in like she had just floated through a field of daisies

for a cosmetic commercial. I waited for her smile to fade, for her to say she hurt inside. We knew each other well enough. But Ann's unrealistic temperament never ended. "Well, praise the Lord that one's over," was the closest she came to admitting she felt any strain at all.

Sitting in the coffee shop that morning across from Ann, I wondered if she lived in the same world I did. I felt like saying: *Ann, please tell me how you feel beneath that smile. Won't you admit you're tired and thought the test was terrible? At least admit you cried about your sister's baby and that you're lonely without letters from Ron. Let me know you're human and not some smiling mannequin behind a showcase Christianity. Don't tell me everything's fine when it isn't.*

When I left Ann that day in the coffee shop, I had an uneasy feeling about her. And as long as I had known her, everything was fine. I don't know if her smile ever soured or her world ever went gray.

It seems to me that somewhere between Margaret's valleys and Ann's eternal mountaintop there must be a plane where happy, realistic living can take place. I've read about a man who found that balance.

SUMMER SPIRIT

His circumstances were about as depressing as possible. Imprisoned. Four unchanging walls. Separation from friends. Chained night and day to a prison guard. Aside from a few visitors, his only communication with the outside world was by letter.

Though in devastating circumstances, this man, the apostle Paul, still saw the good, the positive, in his situation. He wrote to the church at Philippi: "All my prayers are full of praise to God for your help. God is here with me . . . I'm healthy and content. I'm going to keep on being glad because I know, whether I live or die, God is going to work this out for my good."

Obviously, Paul didn't sit in his cell and conduct a private pity party. He didn't pretend he was sitting on a springtime mountaintop counting daisy petals either. He admitted in the same letter that everything was not "fine": "I'm lonely for you. Some of the people I thought were friends have turned out to be phony. I know I'm going to die and be with God, but I want to stay with you. I'm in the middle of an intense struggle. Pray for me."

Paul was confident in God's ultimate control over his circumstances, but he was emotionally honest with his friends. There was a balance in Paul's attitude I want to keep in mind when I catch myself leaning toward either of the Margaret/Ann extremes.

Photo by Jean-Claude Lejeune

SELF

SELF

Jay Kesler

George was a terrific person. He could tell jokes that made everybody laugh, he was good at sports, and people liked him. In fact, everybody liked George except George. I know, because I talked to him a lot, and when you really got under the surface you could tell. He was full of self-doubt. He hated looking in the mirror.

Why? George had a nose that took up nearly a third of his face. You wouldn't necessarily call it ugly—but you would certainly call it big. And when George thought about himself, the first thing that came to mind was that nose. He couldn't recall any of his good qualities; all he could think of was that big, ugly (in his eyes) schnozzola.

He is not alone. If God advertised that he'd do alterations at such and such a place, the waiting line would stretch across the continent. If you're like most people, you probably have something you don't like about yourself: acne, a big mouth, curly hair, straight hair, a lack of athletic ability, or a body that is too tall, short, fat, or skinny.

Maybe you have a legitimate personal problem that needs treatment. Or maybe you don't. But the bigger question is this: *How does your personal problem affect your total view of yourself?*

It's not good for you to dislike yourself; it's depressing, and what's more, it insults God, because God is the one who made you. When you look in the mirror and make a face, you're making a face at God.

But knowing that doesn't always help. The feelings are still there. God made you, all right, but you're probably wondering why he didn't do a better job. How can you learn to live with yourself?

Vive la Difference

The first thing to understand is why God made you the way he did. Why did God make tall people and short people, thin people and wide people, active people and slow people, talkative people and quiet people? Why did God make big noses?

The Scripture says that when God looked at the world he'd made, he said it was good. He didn't say, "The handsome things are good." All of it was good! If you forget yourself for a while, you see this is true. Differences are what make people interesting, and some have made fortunes in entertainment or athletics with very unusual physical qualities.

Then look at a magazine, like *Glamour,* in which every picture fits someone's ideal standards of beauty. What's the result? A plastic sameness that makes it impossible even to remember the girl's faces. When everyone's the same, everyone gets lost.

God could have made people like Henry Ford made cars: every one the same. It probably would have been more efficient, and certainly no one would have complained about getting a bad deal. But God did exactly the opposite. How many variables are there? Noses, mouths, eyes, ears, skin, height, weight, and so on. In the same way the telephone company takes seven digits and makes a different combination for everybody, God uses those differences to make us so that there are no two people on earth exactly alike.

Maybe you've never wondered why God made you different from anyone else, because it's easy to take your uniqueness for granted. But there's a message in all of our differences, and the message is, God loves variety. He made everyone different because he thought we deserved to be different. He doesn't work only with masses of people, like a statistical sociologist; he works with individuals. He likes individuality.

How can you say God made a mistake when he made you? What makes you think God flubbed up or failed when he didn't make you the All-American Everything? You are important and special to him no matter

31

how ugly or unlovable you think you are. And he wants you to view yourself in the same way he does.

Spiritual Kamikaze

Some people will tell you the Bible says just the opposite. They look at Galatians 2:20—"I have been crucified with Christ and I no longer live, but Christ lives in me"—and they think that means you ought to be a spiritual Kamikaze. They figure the best Christians are those who crawl out from between the mattress and the springs and say, "I'm nothing. I'm a worm. I can't do it. Whatever it is you want, I can't do it." They try to destroy self-respect, and whenever they feel proud of something they were part of, they have to hide that feeling.

The trouble is, these people seem phony. No matter how hard they try, they don't show genuine humility. It's all a put-on. They're just trying to look good in another way, as if to say, "I bet I'm twice as humble as you are."

The Bible says the humble person is the honest person. You're not supposed to think of yourself more highly than you deserve, and you're to think of others before yourself. But that doesn't mean you make yourself into a worm. If God wanted you to be a worm, he wouldn't have had any trouble making you one. He's very good at worms.

Among the problems this worm-attitude creates is that people who can't accept themselves usually have trouble relating to others. Jesus said we should love our neighbor as we love ourselves—and if we don't love ourselves, how can we love our neighbor?

But Jesus can change this worm-attitude. When we accept his forgiveness he wipes out our sin so that we're not only acceptable to *him* but also acceptable to *ourselves*. God has made us whole again, and no matter how many times we mess up our lives, he continues to renew us. Because of that, we can love ourselves, and we can begin to really love others, too.

Loving yourself can be carried to an unhealthy extreme, where it becomes selfish—expecting the whole world to be tailored to your liking. But avoiding selfishness doesn't mean kicking your *self* out of the picture. You aren't to destroy your *self:* you're to use it to serve God.

Every attribute has two sides. A childish person is immature

The Campus Life Guide

and not adult in manner, but a child-like person is trustful, candid, and loving. God wants to eliminate selfishness in us, but self-acceptance and self-respect are traits that he wants to develop in a healthy and positive way.

Whose Standard?

There have been commercials on television for tires that have a "computer-designed tread." Actually, no computer ever designed a tire tread without a program created by some smart people. The commercial should say, "Designed by some of the smartest people in the world with the help of a computer." Because of messages like these, you watch television and find out you're not as smart as a computer. You pick up a magazine and realize your body doesn't come up to the *Vogue* or *Sports Illustrated* standard. You go to school and find out you're not good enough to make the most popular crowd. When you stop to think about it, the world's standards of acceptance are much harder to meet than Jesus' standards. You never really make the world's standards, there's always one more rung on the ladder of success. But you're

already accepted by Jesus no matter who you are.

The Christian must have a different standard. If you take your temperature with a thermometer that's inaccurate, you may find you have the world's worst temperature. That's why getting rid of the world's "thermometer"—the standards set by the world and the kids at school—and measuring yourself by God's standard are essential. God's standard is that a person is successful not by his or her appearance or ability but by what is in the heart.

As you read the Bible you find that God's standards are repeatedly stressed. You learn to live by them because you're saturated with an understanding of them every day. Then when you pray you thank God for what he's done—including making you the way you are and making your world the way it is. You realize as you pray and meditate that God cares about you—the unique, invaluable *you*. This is why your personal time with God and his Word are essential.

You're Okay

It may surprise you to realize that accepting yourself is not the sort of thing you can do alone.

You need help from other Christians, too. Christians should bear each other's burdens, love each other, point out each other's good qualities.

This kind of mutual support can really help to reinforce God's standards of measurement in our lives. And it helps us feel better about ourselves.

Try an experiment: Instead of always complaining to each other about how your lives aren't all they could be, try building each other up. Make a point of telling your Christian friends what you like about them. They are, Scripture says, God's gifts to you. Let them know that by the standards of Christ they are tremendous people. You may find that when you help them believe in themselves, their performance as Christians improves. And if they do the same to you, you'll see a difference in yourself as well.

The Rose Garden

I once had a very flowery way of talking about the value of each person. I would talk about man as the pinnacle of God's creation, and I'd illustrate it with the idea of the plant world as a pyramid. At the bottom are the algae and the lichens, up a little further are the weeds and grasses, and at the top you find the crowning achievement: the rose. It's very fragile, beautiful, and complex. All the other plants are great, but the rose is something very, very special.

Mankind is the finest thing God has made. We're like the rose—the very top. God cared so much about us he sent his son to die for us.

Once after I had given this speech, a polite elderly gentleman asked me how much I knew about roses. I said I didn't know too much, really.

"Well," he said, "I do." He'd been raising prize-winning roses for many years. "You know," he said, "if you leave a rose just as God created it, it's a pretty small thing. You get a little flower and a lot of thorns. But when you cooperate with God, as rose-fanciers do, then you really get something. You get the roses that people really love, in all their wild variation of color and beauty."

He was saying there's more to life than accepting the fact that God made us and thinks we're tremendous. That's important—very important. But if you start with self-acceptance, you have to move on to self-improvement. God loves you exactly the way you are, but there are some things he would like to see you change. When you work with him at changing them you will become the person he intends you to be. You become like a beautiful, cultured rose.

I once counseled a girl who was obese, and when she came to talk to me I hardly had to say a word. Her story came pouring out, problem after problem. Her pastor couldn't help her; he just got nervous when she came around. Her folks didn't love her and were always picking on her. Teachers made fun of her in front of other kids at school. She showed me a scar on her forehead where her dad had hit her once—he was always hitting her.

After an hour of listening, I said something that I would not usually say to someone I didn't know well. "Elaine, how many of your problems are directly related to the fact that you're about a hundred pounds overweight?"

She stopped cold. She sat stunned for a moment and then she started to cry. She cried and cried, and I began to wonder if I should have said it. She paused for a moment, then looked up at me and stammered, "You know, nobody ever said anything like that to me before."

"I'm not a medical doctor," I said. "I don't know a thing about medicine. But I'd suggest you go to a doctor and get a diet. And then you stick to it."

Then I added, "There is one thing I can do to help. I can be your friend. You can write to me and tell me how you're doing, and I'll write and encourage you along."

For three years she wrote me every week. "Lost a pound." "Gained two." "Lost five." "Gained three." Slowly, painfully, she made progress.

About six months after we started on the project, she wrote, "Jay, I've been lying to you. My dad isn't really that bad a person. Neither is my pastor or the kids at school. The truth is, I hated myself so badly that I found myself blaming these other people."

That's typical of all of us. *What we can't stand in ourselves we blame on other people.* If you feel like that, there are two messages God has for you, the same two messages Elaine had to learn. The first is that *God loves you, no matter who you are*—"ugly" or good-looking. His standards are a lot different from the world's. If you're not quite like everybody else, it's because he didn't want you like everybody else.

The other message is that if your problems are something you can solve, as Elaine's were, then God wants to lovingly and firmly help you solve them. It isn't that he'll love you more then. He already loves you more than you can imagine, just as you are. But because he loves you, *he wants you to be all you can be.*

ROAD TO SOMEWHERE

Steve Lawhead

I was fat. The plain truth. None of the semipolite euphemisms—portly, husky, stout, big-boned, plump— would diminish the fact that I was obese in the extreme. And when you're seventeen and fat and desperately trying to slink invisibly through high school, you don't have many friends— at least not the kind of friends you would like to have.

My friends were the people "cool" kids didn't like to have around. Rejects.

There was a guy who was an asthmatic, a spindle of a person who wheezed his way through P.E. and couldn't do anything magical on a football field. There was a squat kid—the shortest person in the class. He had a baby face and everyone called him Rocky the Flying Squirrel (when they noticed him at all). He read science like a fanatic and played chess the same way—I know because I played chess with him. There were others who, because of some physical stigma or personal oddity, didn't fit in. Like the guy named Walter Withers (known to all as "Wilt") whose only social handicap aside from his name what that he was just *different*.

These were not the people I would have preferred to have as friends . . . at the time. In high school my one driving desire was to be liked and accepted. All I wanted was to walk into a crowded room, have someone call out my name, and instantly be ushered into a close-knit fellowship; to go out with the guys on Friday nights; to be able to call up any girl I wished, ask for a date, and have her accept. That's all I wanted.

It never happened.

But something was happening just the same. Something I wasn't aware of then. I was discovering a few of the things in life that were real and valuable, things that sound a little corny when you talk about them, but are not less important because of that. I was learning the value of friendships based on mutual trust and understanding rather than on who

*All I wanted was to walk into a crowded room,
and have someone call out my name.*

had the raciest car or could run a 440 in 60 seconds. And because each of us was often put down and made fun of, I learned the virtue of accepting others and treating them as I liked to be treated myself.

To the slick, well-polished kids in our school, we may have seemed an ungainly group of miscast characters. But we each had our own hopes and ambitions. And, forced together in common misery, we grew to appreciate each others' talents and abilities.

The skinny asthmatic, for instance, was a first-rate bowler. By the time he was a senior, he had bowled three perfect games, was traveling to distant tournaments, and had won a roomful of trophies. The kid called Rocky went on to study botany, earned a Ph.D., and has discovered several new species of aquatic plants; some of them are even named after him. Wilt had a natural talent in drama and a humorous bent. He began writing funny one-acts and won a college scholarship in drama. The last time I saw him he was performing a one-man show of several of his plays and was well

on his way to becoming another Neil Simon.

These accomplishments may not stop people in the streets; they're not the stuff Nobel prizes are made of. But that's not really the point. It wasn't that we were better than anyone else, but that we had value as persons even though it may not have been recognized and applauded by the trend-setters.

Also, our enforced segregation gave us opportunities to develop talents and interests that we probably wouldn't have developed any other way. I know this was true for me. Since my Friday nights were hardly grist for Hollywood's gossip mills, I found time and energy to devote to writing and painting—two endless sources of pleasure and fulfillment. It's hard now to see how those bleak weekends could have been better spent; I wouldn't trade one of those "empty" Friday nights for the memory of a date with any prom queen.

I n a way, my dissatisfaction with my life drove me to depend upon my inner self (my outer self wasn't all that

It wasn't that we were better than anyone else, but that we had value as persons.

dependable) and to develop inner strength. I know if I'd been president of my senior class I'd have spent a lot more time worrying about school politics than preparing for a career.

I lost that extra weight eventually. Pared down to an acceptable size, I learned that all the time and experience I considered wasted and worthless had been working together to make me into the person I wanted to be.

Of course, looking back is easy; it's plain to see where the road has led you. But while you're plodding along, it's often hard to believe you're going anywhere at all—or that there even *is* a road. The times I felt worthless were hard for me. I doubt if it would have made any difference if someone had told me, "Don't feel bad; God can use all this. You'll see." But for me it was true nonetheless—the road was leading somewhere.

OUT OF MY LEAGUE

Ruth Senter

"I can't go in there," I said to myself on that early September day. I stopped at the large, plate-glass doors that opened into a sophisticated jungle of corridors and classrooms. Yesterday had been OK. On my day-before-school-starts inspection tour, I'd pushed open those doors with eager confidence. But now that the halls were filled with kids and the home-room bells were ringing, my courage evaporated.

Keep your mouth shut. I tried desperately to stifle my fears. *That way no one will hear your accent and know you're a country girl from the South.* They might miss my accent, but I knew they wouldn't miss the fact that my brown loafers were last year's style and my blue plaid skirt and white sweater looked like somebody else's leftovers . . . which they were.

These were no second-rate citizens I was going to meet today. I'd been through their yearbook enough times to know this city school had class, style, size. "Big fish in a little pond. That's what you've been," my dad had said. "Now you're a minnow in the ocean."

This day, as I walked toward that academic sea, I wished for my little pond where all had been safe and secure. There people knew me and liked me. There *everyone* said "y'all." Here everything was different. And I felt third-class.

"God, I need a shot of courage," I whispered as I pushed open the heavy glass doors.

At first my mind couldn't focus on details. A collage of faces whirled before me. I pointed myself in the right direction and drifted with the tide, hoping I could slip by without anyone noticing. As long as they didn't know me, at least they couldn't reject me.

Then it happened. Right in front of the swinging doors that opened into the library. I saw a face I recognized. Before I could stop myself I blurted out, "Hi. Aren't you Claudia White? You play hockey and you're a varsity cheerleader."

OUT OF MY LEAGUE

Claudia searched my face but have no sign of recognition.

"You don't know me. I'm new. I found you in the yearbook. The school sent me a copy before we moved. Guess your face stood out." My words tumbled over each other.

Claudia smiled. Instantly a wall went down. I knew her name. Who doesn't respond when one hears her name called? I felt a surge of courage. Somehow things didn't seem nearly so scary when I could call someone by name. I determined I would memorize the entire yearbook if I needed to.

I walked home from school that day with a lot of insecurities still fluttering around inside. I knew the year would be tough. I was way behind my class in most subjects. Dad was without a job; I'd be wearing my outdated loafers for a long time. I was still the new kid in town with plenty of reasons to feel insecure. And I did.

I remember a sunny April afternoon the same year I moved to that new school. I was the only person in sight as I walked down Grant Street toward home, but I was imagining the whole

school watching me, sitting on the bleachers laughing at me. I felt about three foot one; my self-esteem had shrunk to midget proportions.

It was all because of a tennis match, the first of the season. Why hadn't I gotten the hint the first day of practice? Just because my friend's dad owned a private court that I could practice on any time I pleased, and just because my friend was the best player on the team didn't mean I was going to become a tennis player by osmosis. I should have known I was not the tennis type.

From the first volley my game had gone downhill. I kept checking the bleachers to see who was noticing. I did a public commentary on my every move— "Should have had that one. Dumb move. Too slow. Wrist broke. Racket too high." I guess I wanted to be sure everyone knew that I knew I was doing it wrong.

My partner yelled words of encouragement to me from time to time, but I barely heard them. *She feels sorry for me. Too bad I have to ruin her game, too,* I thought as I watched Karla gracefully tuck a backhand over the net and drop it next to the line. Perfect court position. Out of everyone's

OUT OF MY LEAGUE

reach. Definitely out of my league.

By the time the doubles match was over, my confidence had been wiped out. "Call me klutz. Can't do anything." I sang my tennis blues to my mom when I got home. "If I were the type of person who could relax I might have had half a chance. Couldn't relax about the chem exam this morning either. Talked myself right into a splitting headache. Couldn't even remember one carbon compound. Guess I'm just an uptight person."

My mom was not impressed with my logic. She tried to encourage me and finally ended our discussion by saying, "Promise me one thing. Next time you walk out on that court, remember the award of excellence you won in creative writing."

It made no sense at all. I could find no link whatsoever between winning a creative writing contest and smashing a tennis ball within the appropriate white lines. But over the years I have caught on to my mother's strategy: When your confidence is so low it doesn't register, it helps to remember the things you do well.

I never did break any tennis records. In fact, I eventually gave up tennis for drama. But my mother's advice about confidence has given me the courage to pick up my tennis racket every now and then and enjoy a game.

Another confidence-building exercise for me has been to seize any opportunity to succeed at something new.

"Trust yourself," my dad used to say. "See what needs to be done, then get to work and do it." I knew what needed to be done the minute I heard the minor explosion coming from my back left tire. But there were many reasons why I should not change that tire myself. That was a man's job. Not only was I female, but a non-mechanical type of female, and I just wasn't cut out for car lifting, I told myself.

My dad had taught me how to change a tire, so that I knew how to do it, but I'd never seen any of my girlfriends changing a tire. Besides, I knew help was just a quarter mile away at the corner Texaco station. I started my jog toward the station but something in my mind pulled me back. I turned around, unlocked the trunk, took a deep breath, pulled out the jack, and set to work.

By the time the last lug was

OUT OF MY LEAGUE

tightened securely in place and my car was resting firmly on four full tires again, my confidence had skyrocketed. I felt like I could tackle the world. I had succeeded at something I thought I never could do.

Life is full of tires waiting to be fixed, high walls to be scaled, and closed doors to be opened. The impossibilities sometimes scare me—send me running the other direction. But God has an alternate plan of action in mind for me. "I want to remind you," he says, "to stir into flame the strength and boldness that is in you . . . for the Holy Spirit, God's gift, does not want you to be afraid . . . but to be wise and strong . . ." (2 Timothy 1:6–7, *The Living Bible*).

The confidence-building strategies I've learned—focusing on others, remembering the things I do well, and tackling new challenges—often help. But sometimes what confidence boils down to is simply remembering the resources of God that are available to me. With the God of creation at work in my life, I have no good reason to say "I can't."

Photo by Verne Becker

LONELINESS

LONELINESS

Jay Kesler

Not long ago I met a girl with very deep problems. Joan was considering suicide.

She told me it began with feeling lonely. She was going through a lot of things, and sometimes she felt like no one understood her or liked her. She tended to stay around the house and often acted moody. Her mother said, "There must be something wrong with you," and started telling Joan she ought to see a counselor. That may not have been a bad idea, but to Joan only sick people saw counselors. So her mother's comment reinforced the notion that because she felt lonely, she was sick. And that idea got stronger and stronger, until she was ready to commit the ultimate act of self-destruction.

I talked to Joan for a long time and stressed one fact again and again—everybody is lonely. It's the most normal thing in the world. Nearly all humans feel rejected and lonely at times, even in crowds, and nearly all humans want to go off alone sometimes and work things out in their own heads.

Loneliness, almost by definition, feeds on itself. Lonely feelings make you burrow into yourself, make you look at the rest of the world as though it's very different from you. And that makes your loneliness worse.

Most of the lonely people I've talked to are afraid. They're worried that other people won't accept them. They have a set of assumptions about what other people think of them; they tend to say, "I know what they're thinking." Consequently, they isolate themselves.

But the assumptions are usually way off; most of those other people aren't self-assured either. Most of them aren't out to look down on people, and the truth is, most of *them* are as lonely and miserable as you are. Even the people who make a habit of putting you down most likely don't really hate you. They've got problems of their own, and you just happen to be in the way when they look for someone to snub. They're using put-downs and fake self-confidence (at least sometimes) as defense mechanisms to hide their own loneliness.

If you will examine and analyze your assumptions about other people, I think you'll find they're not based on much evidence. How do you know what they think of you? Look at your feelings, and then start assuming other people feel exactly the same way. You want a friend? Okay, assume they want a friend, and you'll be right ninety percent of the time. You like most people? So does ninety percent of the world, which means most people probably like you. Try going through a day at school just assuming that every-

one you know basically likes and admires you. Chances are very good that the evidence in favor of that assumption will pile up. What if someone doesn't respond to that assumption? He's only among the ten percent.

But how do you find the courage and self-confidence to act on your new set of assumptions?

There's a famous story about a man who tried to peel an onion. He kept peeling layer after layer, looking for the real onion inside. Only after he'd taken off every layer did he realize that an onion is all peel. There is no core, no real fruit inside.

Many times I feel like that's a symbol of my life. I'm all peel; when you've stripped away all my attitudes and relationships, there's nothing left. And then it's very simple to feel lonely and it's very hard to be outgoing. If I'm rejected, what have I got left over? There's no core.

That's one of the primary reasons I'm a Christian. Christ is the core of my life and the one solid thing that exists in my world. He will never leave me or forsake me. He will stay with me no matter what I am. He accepts me, unconditionally.

With that as a basis, my human relationships become a kind of bonus. I'm not risking everything when I meet someone. A lot of kids never risk themselves in relationships, because, subconsciously, they feel that if things go wrong they've lost everything. A Christian doesn't have to feel that way, because Christ is always a friend who sticks closer than a brother.

And Jesus knows how you feel. He took the first and biggest risk of rejection by coming into our world without any armor to protect him. He came as a normal human being, without any flashing signs that said, "I'm God." He came and experienced total rejection. He wants to be with you when you take the same kind of risks while reaching out to other people, and you can always fall back on him.

I Need Friends

Last week a fellow came up to me and said, "I've never had a date. I don't feel I've ever had a friend. I've always felt like everyone was too busy for me. I always stand at the edge of conversations, and people never include me. I feel completely alone, completely rejected, and I don't know how to handle it."

So we talked about his problems. He knew Christ and said he felt close to him, but he said,

"That's not enough. I need more in life. I need people to like me."

And I had to agree with him. God didn't create us to be hermits. He made us with personality, with the capacity for friendship and loyalty, and because of that capacity for friendship, we feel lonely when we don't have friends.

But loneliness has a way of urging us to overcome it; it naturally pushes us toward other people so that we can once again experience the friendship and intimacy God created us for. Of course, that doesn't mean we make friends easily or automatically. We have to work at it.

Do you want to be accepted? Work at accepting people. Do you feel people reject you? Work at not giving other people signs of rejection every time they try to find a way into your friendship. I'm talking about the Golden Rule here—do unto others as you want them to do to you. That's not just a trite, moralistic phrase; it's a practical way of going about life. It works. People who practice it tend to have fewer troubles relating to other people, and they end up happier.

When you start applying the Golden Rule as a way of opening your life to friendship, you start by listening a lot. You ask questions. You try to find whether there is some area of another person's life he wants to talk about—not just problems, but areas where he really has some confidence. Listening is one of the basic rules of conversation, but it's something that a lot of lonely people don't understand. They (understandably) want to talk, but if they do all the talking, the person who's listening soon gets tired of it. The friendship has to be two-way: both of you need time to talk and time to listen.

It's an unrealistic goal to expect to be popular with everyone overnight, and I doubt it's all that desirable. Having a lot of not-so-close friends is nice, but they may not keep you from feeling lonely. What's much more important is to have one or two very close friends with whom you can be completely honest. And that's a rare thing— it's a very happy man or woman who has even one.

But again, in trying to develop that close friendship, most lonely people make the wrong assumptions. They don't understand that friendship is based on sharing weakness, not strength. They try to impress people with how neat they are and are surprised when that doesn't work. They think the football hero and the basketball hero have friends just because they're strong. But those people, if their popularity is genuine, probably make friends the same way everyone else does—by sharing weakness.

It's not the kind of sharing you do all the time or that you do with someone you just met. You do it very carefully and very tenderly. You have to be sensitive to the right time, and you must be open for the other person to share something with you if he or she wants to.

Of course, very lonely people often want to go out and become close friends with the most popular and vivacious people. It seldom happens. For one thing, the sharing would be unequal. If you're shy and insecure, it's very difficult to get the courage to share even a small personal fear or weakness. It may seem like nothing at all to the self-confident kid who's so secure that he can talk about his complexion or about sex without batting an eye. Sharing, if it's to build deep friendship, should be something equal. You have to start with people more or less like yourself. Eventually you'll learn to feel comfortable with a wider group of people.

The Ugly and Unlovely

Okay, you say, so I follow your advice. I end up with a bunch of friends who are ugly, incapable, and unlovely. I spend time with other lonely people. I'm in a group all right, but it's a group that nobody cares about.

There's something wrong with that line of thinking. It ranks people in status according to how athletic they are or how good-looking. But as I understand it, young people say again and again that you can't judge a person by how he looks, that people who don't achieve the *important* things aren't worthless, that everybody's different and has to find his own way. Kids say, "It isn't important what you look like, it's what you are."

But do you really believe that? Probably not. When you go looking for friends, you want one of the really well-liked, well-thought-of people to notice you. It comes down to status, just like it does when the older generation judges people by their clothes or how much money they make.

Personally, I've found those values to be worthless in the long haul. Many people who seem to have nothing to offer turn out to be my most treasured friends. And some people who seem to have all the status often turn out to have areas of their lives that are ugly and unlovely. Nobody is a zero. Why? Frequently, it's because they got status through their genes. The girl had a pretty face or the guy had a great body or they were born into the right families. That made them liked. But when the bodies had gone downhill, what was left? They'd never developed the kind of inner strength that went beyond those things.

To develop real strength as a person, start where you are. If you're talented in something, develop that. Start building friendships with people you can relate to as peers. Treat everybody the way you want them to treat you. And learn to expect that ninety percent of the world is as lonely and hungry for friendship as you are.

If you do that, you're going to find you're rarely lonely. You will find you can enter different groups and feel at ease. You will have one or two intimate friends with whom you can share anything about yourself. Your relationship with Jesus will be deep and strong, and you will be able to risk rejection from people because you're sure of his support.

Then what do you do?

You begin to reach out to include other people.

It was once common to describe people who were really at the top as *exclusive*. It's not a current word, but it still describes the way a lot of the most popular people function; they stay at the top by excluding others. George Bernard Shaw said once that *exclusive* is the ugliest word in the English language. I think I agree. I think the Bible would agree.

Your Christian responsibility is this: whenever you're with a group that's forming a little circle, and you see someone standing on the edge, move toward them and invite them into the circle. No Christian should ever allow people to stand outside the circle. You've got to break the circle, physically and symbolically. Step back and say, "Join us." If you're going somewhere, say, "Why don't you come along?" Pretty soon you find a spirit developing in yourself and even in your group. You're inclusive instead of exclusive. If more Christians were like that, there would be fewer lonely people.

TAKING RISKS

Philip Yancey

Heather had loneliness stamped all over her. She had several strikes against her from the start. Because of a scalp infection, her hair came out in clumps when she brushed it. She would anxiously pull on it and more would come out. Her complexion wasn't the greatest. I knew Heather through her brother Mark, my tennis partner, who told me his sister would stand in front of the mirror for thirty minutes at a stretch, just staring and worrying.

Heather flunked a college speech class when she refused to stand in front of the class to talk. In most classes she would sit in the last row and spend her time doodling or leafing through magazines. She looked fatigued and pale, and people wondered whether she had been taking drugs.

I tried to talk to Heather when we would sit on Mark's back porch after playing tennis, drinking iced tea. But whenever I asked Heather a question, she gave one-word responses like "Yeh" or "Dunno." Carrying on a conversation like that was just too much work for me.

Heather soon began working the night shift in a factory, and I rarely saw her. When I visited Mark, Heather was always in her bedroom, shades drawn, sleeping.

Heather's case is extreme, but it is an example of the most common type of loneliness: the kind that stems from a poor view of self. In Heather's case the problems were poor conversational skills and fears about her physical appearance. Even her friendly, outgoing brother Mark probably made her feel inferior by contrast. Other reasons for this feeling in someone could be a nagging parent, a speech defect, a failure to attract dates. In any case, a person starts wondering, *What's wrong with me? I don't seem to fit in. No one cares about me. There must be something unlikable about me.* The natural reaction is to tunnel back inside, making it even harder for people to approach him or her.

The only cure for Heather or anyone afflicted with loneliness is to relax those barriers a little, open up, and take some risks with other people. When I am lonely, I am afraid to show others what I am really like for fear he or she will reject me. I think I need to show a confident, brash front for people to like me. But in reality, the opposite is true: people like to see someone honest and vulnerable. When I muster the courage to talk on a deep level with a friend, he almost always responds gratefully.

I wanted to be Heather's friend. But because she did not let me in on what was going on inside her—her tastes, her hobbies, her job, her favorite books and movies—we couldn't even carry on a conversation.

As I write this, I feel stabs of guilt because I think of all the times I have failed to open up to other people when I am lonely. Taking risks is hard, especially when you have been badly wounded by someone . . . and yet it is the only answer.

Counselor Paul Tournier ultimately found that there was only one source for the strength that would permit honesty and openness: God. When God's son Jesus was on earth, he seemed especially attracted to lonely people: tax collectors like Matthew and Zaccheus, fishermen who spent all day in boats away from others, a Samaritan woman shunned by decent people. He approached all those people with respect and told them they could be made whole by following him and experiencing for themselves God's love. God has the absolute right to tell us we are worthwhile, because he designed us even before we were born. Jesus proved how much he loved us by giving his life for us.

It is difficult for me to pick up a Bible and start reading when I am feeling lonely. I prefer to wallow in my loneliness. But whenever I do read the Bible I am reminded on every page how much God cares. He is there, and he is willing to meet us, if we let him.

Christianity asks me to do a strange thing. Normally I like to boast about my strengths to everyone around me so they will be impressed. I instinctively hide my weaknesses and failings so that I will look good among others. Jesus said that's all backward. I should learn humility,

Taking risks is hard, especially when you have been badly wounded by someone.

thinking about other people's strengths and not my own. And I should share my weaknesses and fears with him and with others. If I bottle them up, they will ferment inside me until they poison me; but if I release them, sharing openly with others, the cure is at hand.

THE LONELY QUIET

Jim Long

Sometimes I feel isolated,
 completely alone,
 as if I am entombed
in a plexiglass shell.
I can look out, and
others can look in.
But we are separated.

The word loneliness
used to suggest only solitude,
no one else around.
And sometimes it is like that:
I feel as if I am flying solo
through an empty world.

But often I am surrounded by
 people who
swirl around me
like a Tilt-O-Whirl ride
at a shopping-center carnival.
I reach out to touch them, only
to feel my knuckles bang against
the plexiglass shell.
Or I speak and my voice
 ricochets
off clear plastic,
echoing back at me
much like it would in a
large auditorium with poor
 acoustics.
So I turn my head and listen
 intently—
at least I can tune in on
the conversations around me.
But the voices are muffled,
 distant.
Again I am merely the spectator
behind the shield.

Some people tell me
 I should not have lonely
 feelings.
I should climb out of my shell,
as if I can instantaneously
melt the plastic
or *will* the shell to shatter.
Don't they understand the
 feeling?
Haven't they ever,
even once,
felt my confining hollowness?

People tell me I am never
 alone, that
even in this lonely shell,
I have God.
But that doesn't offer me much
 comfort.
For while I know God is always
 with me,
I can't see him:
I can't converse with him
and hear his response.
Nor can I imagine *him* telling me,
"You have God, that's enough."

55

Photo by Verne E

An ancient story strikes
me:
In my mind I hear
God's voice.
He merely speaks
and the galaxies appear.
And he says it's good.
He speaks and the earth
is filled with vegetation.
Again he says, "Good."
He talks fish into existence,
then wildlife,
then a man, and
Creation is complete.
And he says, "Very good."
But the story continues.
God is touched by the man's
aloneness,
and for the first time he says,
"It is not good." God doesn't
want man to be alone,
so he creates a companion.
Together,
God and these two people
tear down the plexiglass shell.
And throughout time,
again and again,
he has used other people
to help demolish
lonely shells.
So when someone peers into *my*
shell,
gawks at me fighting for space,
and says, "Stop brooding,
God is enough,"
I wonder.

What do I want?
People to pamper me,
to call every lonely feeling a crisis?
Am I merely an emotional
barnacle
looking for a human hull
to cleave to? No.
I am just looking for someone
to care,
someone who knows that
lonely times are normal,
without concluding they
are insignificant.
I could sit back and wait
for that kind of understanding
friend—
prop my feet against the corners
of the shell and lose myself
in self-pity and depression.
But what good would that
do me?
Would anyone think to pull an
emotional corpse out of a
plexiglass coffin?

I can't merely wait.
I will dismantle this cumbersome
shell.
I will push against the plexiglass
panels
until they buckle.
Perhaps some friend will
help me
by prying at the sealed edges
as I lean against them.
That would be easier.
Together we could demolish the
shell
and watch as it dissolved
into a greater friendship
than either of us imagined.

FAILURE

Photo by J. Fred Sharp

FAILURE
Tim Stafford

I turned in my first college essay without trembling. I had breezed through high-school English, and my papers had sometimes been read as examples of what good writing should be. This one may not have been my very best, but I felt sure it would get by.

The next week, before the graded papers were returned, my professor announced he would read one of the essays aloud. I perked my ears up, hoping that my writing would again be used as an example. But this, the professor said, was an example of how *not* to write. He began reading the essay, not mentioning who had written it, but before two lines had been read, I recognized it as mine.

The blood rushed to my ears. I sat frozen, afraid to look around or let anyone know I was the idiot. My staring eyes saw nothing; my head was buzzing with disbelief. I had to listen to the whole essay, and then to the comments. "Stilted." "Repetitive." I am glad that the professor kept my identity a secret, and I could walk out of class with my failure known only to him and me. The sting lingered for a long time.

Yet now I count that day as one of the most significant of my life. As I recovered from the shock, I thought over those safe high-school successes. They had come too easily. What flowed from my pen the first time had been good enough to please my teachers. Now a tough teacher had given me my first writing lesson: you have to work hard to do your best. I spent the rest of that year working hard, trying to learn to write simple, honest sentences that would please my professor. He was not easily pleased, and I didn't get an A from him. But I got an education.

Failure does funny things to people. Some quit. Some withdraw into themselves. Some even have nervous breakdowns. But some get up again and do better.

There is a world of difference between failing and being a failure, but some people seem eager to brand themselves. My father calls it the "zero-one-hundred-percent syndrome." If your life isn't operating at one hundred percent, it must be operating at zero percent.

We're inundated with advice on how to be successful. There are books and courses on how to be a winner. "Work hard, get ahead," is a philosophy that I've heard in one form or another since I was a baby. But hardly anyone has told me how to fail successfully. There are no books on what to do when you've just utterly blown it. "Forget about it," is about the only post-failure advice I've heard. But why forget about it, when I can learn from it?

More and more I see that how one handles failure is a key to success in life and a mark of one's maturity.

There are dangers to success. For example, success can make you overconfident or lazy. That's certainly what happened to me in my high-school English classes. I think the same thing happened to the best athlete in my high school. Monty could probably have lettered in every sport the school offered. He was a natural. But since football was the big sport, that became his specialty. He played quarterback and was named the outstanding football player in the valley. The only trouble was, Monty wasn't very big, and try as he might, he never made it in college football. If he'd practiced other sports where size was less important, we might be watching him on television today. Unfortunately, success lulled him into over-confidence.

Success can also make you afraid of failing. The person who has never failed can become absolutely terrified of not repeating his success. I've known high-school successes who, when they reached college, were so afraid they couldn't measure up to the standard of success that they quit studying and going to class. It was easier for them to explain their poor grades by saying "I didn't study," than to face the possibility that they weren't as smart as their friends in high school had thought.

Others who were popular in high school sensed that in the bigger pond of college they might not impress anyone; they resorted to buttering up people they didn't like, stabbing competitors in the back, or going along with activities they didn't enjoy. Fear of failure brought on by a run of successes can take the joy out of life, replacing it with strain. In contrast, people who have failed a few times know they can survive. They look forward to new opportunities without terror.

I'm not trying to convince you that it's more fun to fail than to succeed. It hurts to fail. But failure can be good for you, if you know how to deal with it.

The trouble is we're protected from experiencing failure. It starts with our parents who, quite naturally, don't want us to get hurt, but too much protection creates a spoiled brat. Didn't everyone have a kid like that in the neighborhood? His poor grades were always the teacher's fault; he lacked friends because the neighbor kids were conceited. When he gave a party, his parents made sure someone came.

All of us tend to baby ourselves the way our parents did. We protect ourselves from failure by not taking risks. We don't try things we may not be good at. We rationalize away the few glaring failures we experience. As a result we miss what failure can do for us if we let it.

As I reflect on my experience in writing class (and plenty of other places), I've learned that failure can help us in several ways. Here are four:

Failure can give you new information. When you succeed at the same old thing, you learn nothing. But failing gives you the opportunity to ask why. If you get a D on a paper, ask the teacher what could make it better. If someone you like seems to be avoiding you, take time to ask what you're doing wrong. If an employer turns you down for a job, ask why.

Failure can push you in a new direction. One of my most devastating failures was being cut from the high-school basketball team. When the coach stuck the list of team members on the bulletin board, I couldn't believe my name wasn't on it. I burned over that for months.

Looking back, however, I can see that I didn't have the body or the skill to be a very good basketball player. I'd given basketball my best, and it wasn't enough; the most I could have hoped for was a seat on the bench. Instead of spending hours practicing a sport I lacked skill at, I was better off concentrating on tennis, a sport I was better at, and having extra hours for friends and books.

Failure can bring freedom. After a failure, when you're no longer protecting a reputation, you're free to try things. You're free to look at yourself in a new way, asking "What really matters to me?"

I felt this way in college when I failed, by my standards, to be the kind of leader that our Christian Inter-Varsity group needed. I had thought I was big stuff, and suddenly I felt as though the newest most immature Christian had more to offer than I did. It was a strange new way to look at the world—as though nobody really needed me or "depended" on me. But in a way it was a relief. I began to ask myself what

I wanted to do. I began to seriously ask God what his plans were for me, instead of assuming that he needed me to be a big organization man.

Failure can bring warmth and vulnerability. Who do you look for when you fail a test? Do you want to talk to the kid who got an A? No, you seek out someone who scored nearer you. When you fail, often your self-protective wall crumbles, and people can see the real person. God can find a way into your life, where before you were too busy for him, too proud to depend on him. Often dramatic failure brings *more* friends, not fewer.

Of course, failure isn't guaranteed to do you good. It depends on you. If a failure crushes you, so that you conclude you *are* a failure rather than a person who failed at one specific thing, then you have failed indeed. If a failure terrifies you so much that you run from it, then fear is controlling you. But if you accept the pain and evaluate what the failure means, you can convert it into one of the best experiences of your life.

THE MEMENTO

Gerald Moore

Coming home from school that dark winter's day so long ago, I was filled with anticipation. I had a new issue of *Sports Illustrated* tucked under my arm and the house to myself. Dad was at work, my sister was away, and Mother wouldn't be home from her new job for an hour. I bounded up the steps, burst into the living room, and flipped on a light.

I was shocked into stillness by what I saw. Mother, pulled into a tight ball with her face in her hands, sat at the far end of the couch. She was crying. I had never seen her cry.

I approached cautiously and touched her shoulder. "Mother?" I said. "What's happened?"

She took a long breath and managed a weak smile. "It's nothing, really. Nothing important. Just that I'm going to lose this new job. I can't type fast enough."

"But you've only been there three days," I said. "You'll catch on." I was repeating a line she had spoken to me a hundred times when I was having trouble learning or doing something important to me.

"No," she said sadly. "There's no time for that. I can't carry my end of the load. I'm making everyone in the office work twice as hard."

"They're just giving you too much work," I said, hoping to find injustice where she saw failure. She was too honest to accept that.

"I always said I could do anything I set my mind to," she said. "And I still think I can in most things. But I can't do this."

I felt helpless and out of place. At age sixteen I still assumed Mother could do anything. Some years before, when we sold our ranch and moved to town, Mother had decided to open a day nursery. She had had no training, but that didn't stand in her way. She sent away for correspondence courses in child care, did the lessons, and in six

At age sixteen I still assumed Mother could do anything.

months was formally qualified for the task. It wasn't long before she had a full enrollment and a waiting list. Parents praised her, and the children proved by their reluctance to leave in the afternoon that she had won their affection. I accepted all this as a perfectly normal instance of Mother's ability.

But neither the nursery nor the motel my parents bought later had provided enough income to send my sister and me to college. I was a high-school sophomore when we sold the motel. In two years I would be ready for college. In three more my sister would want to go. Time was running out and Mother was frantic for ways to save money. It was clear that Dad could do no more than he was doing already—farming eighty acres in addition to holding a full-time job.

L ooking back, I sometimes wonder how much help I deserved. I wanted my parents' time and attention, but it never occurred to me that they might have needs and problems of their own. In fact, I under-

stood nothing of their lives because I looked only at my own.

A few months after we'd sold the motel, Mother arrived home with a used typewriter. It skipped between certain letters and the keyboard was soft. At dinner that night I pronounced the machine a "piece of junk."

"That's all we can afford," Mother said. "It's good enough to learn on." And from that day on, as soon as the table was cleared and the dishes were done, Mother would disappear into her sewing room to practice. The slow tap, tap, tap went on some nights until midnight.

It was nearly Christmas when I heard her tell Dad one night that a good job was available at the radio station. "It would be such interesting work," she said. "But this typing isn't coming along very fast."

"If you want the job, go ask for it," Dad encouraged her.

I was not the least bit surprised or impressed when Mother got the job. But she was ecstatic.

Monday, after her first day of work, I could see that the excitement was gone. Mother looked tired and drawn. I responded by ignoring her.

"I guess we all have to fail sometime,"
Mother said quietly.

Tuesday, Dad made dinner and cleaned the kitchen. Mother stayed in her sewing room, practicing. "Is Mother all right?" I asked Dad.

"She's having a little trouble with her typing," he said. "She needs to practice. I think she'd appreciate it if we all helped out a bit more."

"I already do a lot," I said, immediately on guard.

"I know you do," Dad said evenly. "And you may have to do more. You might just remember that she is working primarily so you can go to college."

I honestly didn't care. In a pique I called a friend and went out to get a Coke. When I came home the house was dark, except for the band of light showing under Mother's door. It seemed to me that her typing had gotten even slower. I wished she would just forget the whole thing.

My shock and embarrassment at finding Mother in tears on Wednesday was a perfect index of how little I understood the pressure on her. Sitting beside her on the couch, I began very slowly to understand.

"I guess we all have to fail sometime," Mother said quietly.

I could sense her pain and the tension of holding back the strong emotions that were interrupted by my arrival. Suddenly, something inside me turned. I reached out and put my arms around her.

She broke then. She put her face against my shoulder and sobbed. I held her close and didn't try to talk. I knew I was doing what I should, what I could, and that it was enough. In that moment, feeling Mother's back racked with emotion, I understood for the first time her vulnerability. She was still my mother, but she was something more: a person like me, capable of fear and hurt and failure. I could feel her pain as she must have felt mine on a thousand occasions when I had sought comfort in her arms.

Then it was over. Wiping away the tears, Mother stood and faced me. "Well, son, I may be a slow typist, but I'm not a parasite, and I won't keep a job I can't do. I'm going to ask tomorrow if I can finish out the week. Then I'll resign."

And that's what she did. Her boss apologized to her, saying that he had underestimated his workload as badly as she had

In seeing her weakness I had not only learned to appreciate her strengths. I had discovered some of my own.

overestimated her typing ability. They parted with mutual respect, he offering a week's pay and she refusing it. A week later Mother took a job selling dry goods at half the salary the radio station had offered. "It's a job I can do," she said simply. But the evening practice sessions on the old green typewriter continued. I had a very different feeling now when I passed her door at night and heard her tapping away. I knew there was something more going on in there than a woman learning to type.

When I left for college two years later, Mother had an office job with better pay and more responsibility. I have to believe that in some strange way she learned as much from her moment of defeat as I did, because several years later, when I had finished school and proudly accepted a job as a newspaper reporter, she had already been a reporter with our hometown paper for six months.

Mother and I never spoke again about the afternoon when she broke down. But more than once, when I failed on a first attempt and was tempted by pride or frustration to scrap something I truly wanted, I would remember her selling dresses while she learned to type. In seeing her weakness I had not only learned to appreciate her strengths. I had discovered some of my own.

Not long ago I helped Mother celebrate her sixty-second birthday. I made dinner for my parents and cleaned up the kitchen afterward. Mother came in to visit while I worked, and I was reminded of the day years before when she had come home with that terrible old typewriter. "By the way," I said, "Whatever happened to that monster typewriter?"

"Oh, I still have it," she said. "It's a memento, you know . . . of the day you realized your mother was human."

I had never guessed that she saw what happened to me that day. I laughed at myself. "Someday," I said, "I wish you would give me that machine."

"I will," she said, "but on one condition."

"What's that?"

"That you never have it fixed. It is nearly impossible to type on

What I remember is not her failure but her courage to go ahead.

that machine and that's the way it served this family best."

I smiled at the thought. "And another thing," she said. "Never put off hugging someone when you feel like it. You may miss the chance forever."

I put my arms around her and hugged her and felt a deep gratitude for that moment, for all the moments of joy she had given me over the years. "Happy birthday!" I said.

The old green typewriter sits in my office now, unrepaired. It *is* a memento, but what it recalls for me is not quite what it recalled for Mother. When I'm having trouble with a story and think about giving up or when I start to feel sorry for myself and think things should be easier for me, I roll a piece of paper into that cranky old machine and type, wor d by painful wor d, just the way Mother did. What I remember then is not her failure but her courage—the courage to go ahead. It's the best memento anyone ever gave me.

NO MATTER WHAT

Tim Stafford

I thought it would be different this time;
I was determined to act the way I wanted,
and that thought made me glad.
But I didn't, and now I'm low.
I want to pick myself up and forget it,
to tell myself,
"So what, you're only human.
You won't fail next time."
Or will I?

Everywhere I look,
I find people wanting more of me than I'm able to give.
There's no escaping it—
life bristles with rules and regulations and expectations.
And if you think you have to measure up
in order to be worth anything,
you may as well admit it:
    You're worthless,
    Worthless.

What does Jesus have to do with us?
Most of my friends think he's just more rules.
Good rules, sure:
"Love your neighbor.
Love God."
But good rules or bad rules,
what's the difference
    if I fail to measure up?

NO MATTER WHAT

But my friends are wrong
    this time.
What Jesus is really about,
    most of all,
is forgiveness and love.
No matter what.

Sit up straight and don't talk back.
Study first, then you can go out.
Did you clean your room?
What were you doing out so late?

My parents have
    rules, and teachers
have rules, and the police
    have rules.
I hate the way they're posted
    on walls or used
(at home) to nag me when I
    feel the worst.
I hate the way my parents
always remind me when
    I'm wrong.

Still, I have to admit
    they're not bad rules.
I know they're "for my own
    good," as they say.
I wish I were the type who
    kept them
all the time, without hassles.

Yesterday I yelled at my sister,
fighting over what to watch on
    TV. And Mom
yelled at me, I yelled back,
    and went outside
to watch the sky. I got cold
    and went
back in. Watching my

sister's show,
I felt like an outcast. I'd failed.
But that failure did not interrupt
    God's love.
He loves me no matter what.

Be cool.
Be mellow.
How come you dress like that?
You really like yourself, don't you?

Yesterday my friend
    Caroline said,
"Why are you always so serious?
Why don't you laugh?"
Later everyone was laughing
    about Eddie Murphy,
and I tried to laugh, but it
    didn't work.
I wanted to say I thought he
    was an idiot.
But I didn't.
Everyone would have thought
I was an idiot if I had.

My friends have things they
    expect me
to measure up to. And if I fail
    to meet their standards,
they don't think I'm so wonder-
    ful. In fact,
they'll punish me the worst way
    possible:
they'll leave me alone.
They'll ignore me.
    But God won't.
His love doesn't depend on
    how I act.

NO MATTER WHAT

He loves me no matter what.
Even when I'm least like him.

Go to church on Sunday.
Love God all the time, more and
more and more.
Have you read your Bible?

I haven't read the Bible
all week.
Last week I did—once or
twice—
but it can't have done me
much good.
I can't even remember where I
was reading from.
And though I tried at times to
pray to God,
my words didn't mean
anything . . .
I started thinking about a test.
And I felt as if God were
frowning on me,
from up high,
so distant his unhappy face was
just a dot.

I felt he couldn't be close
to me. And I knew the church
couldn't be close to me
because I'd failed again.
(Why do I feel most guilty
when I fail in the "religious
things"?)

But God loved me when I
failed,

and when I was far from him
he wasn't far from me. He was
waiting, anxious for me to
accept his love . . .
no matter what.

But what about being
good?
Isn't it important to measure
up to my potential?
To be the kind of friend
I should,
to be the kind of person I
should?
Doesn't that matter to God?

Sure it matters.

But it is not what his love
depends on.
Nothing I could ever do
would be enough to make God
love me.
He just does.

And in turn, love is the only
motive
that will help me be what he
wants,
day after day.
All the other motives for being
good
get tired and worn out.
But when you really love
someone,
it goes on forever.

No matter what.

Photo by Paul Conklin

HABITS

H ABITS

Jim Long

 have a natural tendency," Jeff said, "to go downhill. I start a new job and do well for a while, but after a few months I get worse and worse. I have problems getting along with other people, and I do my job poorly. Some people feel sorry for me—which hurts my pride—and I have a terrible feeling of inadequacy. With me, once things get bad, they only get worse."

Shelley confided, "I always hear about people who *get religion* and—*zap!*—they live *wonderful, problem-free lives,* whatever that is. Me? I'm always telling God, 'I will not swear any more. I will have a clean mind.' Guess how long that lasts?"

"Since I've gone back to school," Mark began, "I've changed my attitude toward God. I've gone back to drugs and smoking. I want to be with the *in* people, but I also want to live like a Christian. A friend said something that really bothered me: 'Once you turn back to your old ways, it gets harder to return to Jesus; you become indifferent.' I'm afraid that has happened to me, and I'm not sure I'll have another chance."

I used to think that how we lived was a simple matter of choice—either doing good or doing bad. Of course, I knew God was involved in the whole thing—patiently waiting for us to come around; eager to forgive if ever we'd own up to our moral hassles. But I assumed the issue was: we must *decide* to be different, then just *do it!*

I've changed my mind. There does have to be that desire to be different. But there is a reason our behavior traps us. There is a reason it's hard to change.

"This is going to sound gross," Lynn cautioned. "For a long time I was terribly obese and it wasn't until recently that I was able to lose a lot of weight. I am 5'2" and now weigh 102 pounds. But I still have an awful obsession with food. I'll go for a few days eating light, well-balanced meals and then I'll just go nuts. I eat all the junk I can find in the fridge, then purposely throw up. I've tried, but I just can't seem to kick this bizarre habit."

B izarre or not, I feel her frustration. It feels terrible to be overpowered by habits. Wouldn't it have been simpler if God had created us incapable of forming them?

It is this capacity to form habits that connects our isolated moral struggles into one continuous, heavy chain. Each individual battle becomes a link. When we repeat an action, it becomes part of us, an automatic response, a habit. The individual links are now connected.

I was waiting in a cafeteria line that snaked its way from the dining hall doors, out across a patio, down a sidewalk, and into the parking lot. Steve, lanky and slightly awkward, ambled up and said he wanted to talk about a problem. So we had lunch together in a corner of the cafeteria.

"I have some thoughts I just can't handle," he ventured. "I've tried to think pure thoughts, but can't. And I'm messed up with a habit I can no longer control. Know what I mean?"

I knew exactly what he meant, and his honesty struck me. I have also been snagged by the hook of runaway thoughts. All habits start with a hook—when that first battle is lost. But if the losing continues, habits become chains. Subsequent links are added until the chains become longer, heavier, stronger. I know, Steve knows, everybody knows what it's like to be tangled up with a habit—adding links like crazy.

I think of Jeff and his *natural downhill tendency* —beginning on a high and degenerating from there. "I start a new job and do well for awhile, then get worse and worse." Each time he failed, it confirmed in his mind that he *was* a failure.

Each time Shelley broke her resolutions and fell back into the old language and thought problems, she found it easier to forget her good intentions the next time. The chain does get stronger.

"Yeah," Steve says, "that's how it is with me. I find myself in the middle of this overwhelming urge and then determine, *I'll quit.* When I can't, it becomes twice as difficult next time."

The repetition and sameness reinforce the habit—same place, same time, same circumstances, same failure—constantly repeated.

Is it even possible to face the full force of a well-established habit and then say, *I think I'll change today?* Who are we kidding? Even our most sincere intentions are no match for highly developed habits.

Linda had been a Christian for six years—"Four of them wasted," she said. "There are so many areas which need improvement. I don't have regular times of prayer and Bible study. I don't tell people at school about Jesus. I don't help around the house. I don't get along with my sister. I pray, 'Lord, what am I doing wrong?' I know what I should be doing, but I just can't do it—or should I say, won't do it. I feel so awful. I am a hypocrite. I want so much to be like other Christians—the ones who seem to glow."

Be like other Christians? Which other Christians? And how do they glow? When it comes to Christians, the apostle Paul was one of the great ones— a *super saint.* Did *he* glow? Didn't he sometimes have the same I'm-just-not-quite-making-it feelings?

"I don't understand myself at all," he said, "for I really want to do what is right, but I can't. I do what I don't want to do—what I hate. When I want to do good, I don't; when I try not to do wrong, I do it anyway. It seems to be a fact of life that when I want to do what is right, I inevitably do what is wrong" (Romans 7:15, 19, 21).

I have seem some people change dramatically. Sometimes new Christians can stop drinking or taking drugs—*immediately.* John was like that. The night he became a Christian he flushed his pills down the toilet and never turned back. He returned to New York and told his family of the change. The apostle Paul said, "When someone becomes a Christian he becomes a brand new person inside. He's not the same anymore. A new life has begun!" (2 Corinthians 5:17).

But shedding habits quickly is the exception. Most often it is a discouraging struggle—with little or no progress. It's almost as if we must go back through the same process we came through in forming the habit. From fighting the problem as a habit, we can progress to skirmishes with wrong actions. From there the battle takes a turn and we do close combat within our minds.

It's a slow battle in which we struggle to destroy one link at a time until we can finally discard the hook that snagged us in the first place.

Progress will probably be uneven. We may just begin to feel proud of our accomplishments and then slip back into the old patterns, back to square one.

It almost seems that our entire lives are taken up adding and subtracting the same chain links. This month we win—a former habit is now nothing more than an occasional action. Three months from now it's a habit again. But it doesn't have to be that way, does it?

Over the years I've come to believe in a simple principle that pertains to habits: the way to overcome bad habits is to put good ones in their places. Could it be that our strong capacity to form habits is a strange gift from God to help us grow? When we do wrong, it can become a habit. Why shouldn't it work for good?

A short passage in the book of Ephesians seems to set forth the same principle. For example, we are to break the habit of lying by speaking truth (substituting one habit for another).

"Stop lying to each other; tell the truth, for we are parts of each other and when we lie to each other we are hurting ourselves" (Ephesians 4:25).

Kleptomania is replaced by its opposite. Don't steal. Work. Give.

"If anyone is stealing he must stop it and begin using those hands of his for honest work so he can give to others in need" (Ephesians 4:28).

The instructions continue: "Don't use bad language. Say only what is good and helpful to those you are talking to" (Ephesians 4:29).

"Stop being mean, bad tempered and angry. Quarreling, harsh words, and dislike of others have no place in your lives. Instead, be kind to each other, tenderhearted, forgiving one another, just as God has forgiven you because you belong to Christ" (Ephesians 4:31-32).

Based on the approach outlined in Ephesians, we can mold a strategy. We will demolish bad habits by replacing them with good. We will face our failures and admit them—specifically. We will study them, and consider their circumstances. Where is the habit practiced? And when? What kind of mood are we in?

We will gather the data and then pinpoint the opposite habit—the good one. We will change what we can change. We will reprogram our minds and swing those new thoughts into action.

Soon, we hope, a new habit will emerge to replace the old. Often we will fail. But when the chains trip us, we can jump up and keep going—liberated, free.

My mind flashes to Tom. He has fallen, but has not jumped up. "I am a very lonely person trying to live in an uncaring world," he assesses himself.

"No one tries to understand me. I've looked for comfort in a close friend who is considered religious. But our friendship has been nothing but game playing and now has ended. I have grown up in the church all my life, but I am fast losing faith in Christianity. Where are all the people who are supposed to be around to lift up those who fall?"

I think of Tom and wish that somehow I could just reach out and tell him, "Hey, Tom! The trap is broken. The chain is shattered. There is a way to change. Jesus introduces us to a whole new style of life—new values, new priorities, new power. And he sticks around to help us pull it off. Say, Tom! Let's learn together how to step out of the broken chains and leave them behind."

TOMORROW TRAP

Tom Kimmel with Gregg Lewis

I felt my entire body stiffen at the sound of a fire alarm clanging in my ear. Jerking to a sitting position, I realized I was still half asleep— the ringing noise was my alarm clock, which said 6:20.

I collapsed on my pillow with a groan. The thought of the next twenty hours seemed too heavy to consider in the early morning darkness, but I couldn't push it far enough from my mind to drift off again.

Expending all the determination I could muster, I rolled out of bed. As I went through the motions of showering and dressing, my body and mind gained momentum. By the time I'd gulped down an almost-instant breakfast and walked out the door, I felt alert enough to drive to campus without endangering the other expressway drivers.

At exactly 7:30 A.M. I arrived at my job in the Georgia Tech computer center. For an hour-and-a-half I worked on the program I'd started the day before. Just before 9 o'clock I pulled my program, grabbed my stack of books, and rushed to my first class of the day.

No sooner had I slid into my seat, when the calculus prof walked into the classroom and headed for the blackboard. Any hope I may have had for an encouraging day disappeared as he listed enough homework to keep Einstein busy for a week. I spent the whole hour wondering when I would find the time.

As I went from calculus to physics class, the day went from bad to worse. When the instructor calmly announced, "The test we had planned for next week on chapters ten through 15 has been rescheduled for tomorrow," I didn't even bother adding my voice to the chorus of protests. I knew it was no use.

The next hour, during psychology, I sat in the back and struggled with the calculus problems. By lunchtime I was so discouraged I tried to forget the morning. I spent an hour eating and talking with two friends who were members of the Christian fraternity where I was a pledge. After lunch I joined

My life was slipping out of my control.

them on the lawn for "a quick game" of Frisbee that stretched to half an hour.

Then I had to rush across town to the Atlantic Stadium where I worked afternoons as a computer programmer. By the end of three hours I sat staring groggily at the display screen trying to think through the next step of the program I was writing for the Atlanta Braves season-ticket package. My boss, noticing my long pause, walked up behind me and said, "You know that program's due tomorrow, don't you, Tom?"

I exploded with frustration. "I know. I know," I snapped. "Just don't worry. I'll get it done." I regretted my sharp words the moment they crossed my lips, but I couldn't seem to help it. My life was slipping out of my control.

After work at the stadium, I dropped back by the campus and checked in at the fraternity house. One of the brothers in the front room stopped me to say he thought prayer had done all it could for the house's hot water heater. "You're going to have to call a plumber. You are the house manager," he added, as if I needed reminding.

"Tomorrow," I said. "Not today." Then I turned and made a quick tour of the house, double-checked the worklist I'd posted at the start of the week, and escaped out the back door before someone else stopped me. I had only an hour-and-a-half before I had to be suited up in the gym for our weekly game in the campus fraternity basketball league.

"Got a big test tomorrow," I told Mom as I walked into the house and retreated to my room. Lying on my bed, I leafed quickly through the physics chapters one time before Mom called me for supper. I silently wolfed down my food.

"I hope you can spare a few minutes from your studying tonight," Mom said. "We've got company coming this week, and I'd like you to get your room into respectable shape."

"Not tonight, Mom," I answered, wiping my mouth with a napkin and pushing away from the table. "I've got a basketball game."

"What about the test? And your room really is. . . ."

"I know," I barked. "I know, just don't worry about it. I'll get it all done . . . tomorrow." I regretted those words, too, even

*My life seemed like one big quicksand pit—
like you see in old Tarzan movies.*

before I saw the look of concern register on Mom's face. But I felt helpless to do anything and had to get going.

After the ball game I drove straight to the catalogue warehouse where I'd found a good-paying, part-time job driving a forklift to move merchandise around. My shift started at 9:30 P.M. and lasted till 2 A.M. I was home by 3 A.M. I opened my physics book, but there was no use. I finally surrendered to the temptation of my bed and fell asleep.

When the ringing started again at 6:20, I knew exactly what it was. But I could only lie there in hopeless exhaustion. My life seemed like one big quicksand pit—like you see in old Tarzan movies. The harder I fought to keep up, the deeper I sank. My semester grades were beyond salvaging. I wasn't doing my best at any of my three jobs. My folks and my friends had spotted the danger signs and tried to warn me. Procrastination had become a habitual defense. I lived with constant tension and irritability.

As I lay there in bed, I wanted to scream, "God, why don't you do something?" I guess as a Christian I felt he should step in and keep me from sinking. But as that thought crossed my mind, I realized it was the first time I'd considered God's relationship to the pressures I felt. I'd shoved him into a corner of my life to make room for everything else. I knew I had to make a definite resolution—to myself and God—that things would change. That *I* would change.

I climbed out of bed and did what one of my friends had suggested weeks before. I listed everything I did each week and the amount of time spent doing each one. I came up with a mind-boggling list: eating, attending classes and church services, keeping score for the basketball games at my old high school, working, playing Frisbee after lunch—over one hundred activities in all. Then I listed the real priorities in my life—things like my faith, my family, education, health, friends and social life. I put my relationship with God at the top and put the other areas in order under that. Then I started filling in items from my activity list onto my priority sheet, under the appropriate catego-

As I put my priority plan into action,
I started finding time for the important things.

ries. Obviously, some things had to go—they just weren't high enough on my priority list. I had to shorten the time spent on some things—no more hour-and-a-half lunches. And I changed other activities from daily to occasional—things like two-on-two basketball with friends.

As I put my priority plan into action over the following weeks, I started finding time for the important things I'd crowded out of my life. For example, instead of lying in bed that extra fifteen or twenty minutes every morning, I got up and spent that time reading my Bible and praying—working on my number one priority for the day. And I began to learn to say "no" or "later" to some of those items on the bottom of my list.

It was too late to salvage last quarter's grades—I ended up with a 0.6 standing for the term. But in the first six weeks of this new term, I've gotten more accomplished than I did all last year. I'm finding that as I control my time, I find more of it to use.

I don't claim total victory in my time battle yet. I have to constantly check myself against my priority list. But I feel there's some control in my life now. And I hope in time that *discipline* will become a habit—as strong a habit as lack of discipline used to be.

WEIGH

TO GO

Karen Wise with Ruth Senter

I didn't exactly look like a skier. But there I stood on top of the slope with my skirt blowing in the wind and the big fur collar of my winter coat pulled up around my face. My friends at the bottom of the hill cheered as the towrope pulled all 180 pounds of me to the top. Even the sprawls on the way up, which I took with great dramatics, were met with applause and catcalls.

The audience grew. Everybody wanted to see the funny fat kid take the slopes in a skirt and fur coat. "Come on, Karen, you can do it," the crowd at the foot of the hill boomed to me. I raised both arms in a victory signal. I knew I could do it. I could make them laugh. I'd been doing it all my life.

This time I was a clown on skis. It was better than sitting alone in the ski lodge while my friends maneuvered gracefully up and down the slopes. If I couldn't stuff myself into a sleek ski outfit or sip hot chocolate in front of a roaring fire with one of the guys I dreamed about at night, then I'd at least get their attention by being funny. Sure, others laughed. But that night I cried myself to sleep. I was tired of providing the entertainment for parties and ski trips, of always being the barrel of laughs. I hated the fat, "funny girl" image I carried everywhere I went.

I didn't want to be weird and different. I wanted to be just like everyone else. I wanted someone to choose me out of the crowd and say, "You are my special friend. I like you because you're you."

But it didn't take me long to realize life was not going to treat me that kindly. By the time I entered junior high, I had reached some painful conclusions about myself: I would always be fat, I would never be beautiful, and I would never have dates like other girls.

As far as I was concerned, I had two choices: I could shrink back into the shadows and disappear among the wallflowers, or I could turn myself into a three-ring circus and laugh my troubles away. I

WEIGH TO GO

chose the circus, and no one ever forgot my performances.

I had an act for all occasions. When I went to a swim party at a friend's house, I jumped into the pool with my clothes on. When our school choir returned from tour, I turned a garbage can upside down, stood on it in the middle of the hall, and led the group in a rousing tune that told the whole school we were back. When drama tryouts came along, I volunteered for such parts as the woman wrestler or the fat lady in pink leotards. When there were no fat, funny parts for me to play, I created my own.

In public I laughed. In private I ate. Food became my comforter for the rejection I felt. At home I ate behind the closed pantry door; at school, in the bathroom stalls. I thought nothing of devouring a dozen donuts in one sitting or thirteen candy bars in one day. No one ever guessed there were six Baby Ruths hidden inside my three-ringed notebook or stuck up the puffy sleeves of my blouse.

I had become the miserable victim of a hopeless cycle. The more I ate, the more I weighed; the more I weighed, the more I hated myself; the more I hated myself, the more I ate. I eventually ate my way to three hundred and forty pounds.

I occasionally attempted to break the cycle. I would determine to stop overeating and hang up my clown outfit, but most of my efforts ended in disaster.

O ne night I was more determined than ever. The party should have been fun—lots of friends and food. Most important, Bob was there.

Bob was good-looking and talented. And he had actually stopped and talked to me in the hall the day before. I promised myself I would prove to him and everyone else at the party that I could be a gracious woman.

I cut the comics. I wore the most slenderizing outfit I owned. I put dainty portions of food on my plate. I tried to sit gracefully with my back straight and my legs crossed like all the slim, classy girls around me. I talked softly and laughed gently. Everyone thought I was sick.

I was feeling good about myself until I went to the counter for a Coke refill. Suddenly I

WEIGH TO GO

panicked. I felt everyone in that room was looking at me. I noticed my fat, stubby fingers reach for the Coke and my puffy wrists that stuck out of too-tight sleeves. I looked across the room at my empty chair. If I wasn't a clown, people must be seeing the real Karen—fat and all. There was nothing to distract them, no cover-ups.

I wanted to disappear. Instead, I hurried back to my chair. But everything seemed stuck in slow motion. I turned to sit, my chair gave way and I sprawled on the floor with a room-shaking crash.

Picking myself up, I stepped back into my clown outfit. I had no choice. Laughter was the only thing that made me feel safe. I cracked jokes about fat people and fragile chairs the rest of the night. Everyone loved it—thinking how well I accepted the fact that I was fat and sometimes broke chairs when I sat on them. But my chair wasn't the only thing shattered that night—so were my hopes and what little ego I had.

After that party it took me months to pick up the pieces. I hated myself for not being able to do anything about my weight, and I hated God for creating me with a weight problem. I felt like one huge mistake.

I began to mistrust people. I was afraid and alone in all my obesity and bitterness. I built a high, hard wall around myself for protection and thought nothing could penetrate it. For years, nothing did.

But one day my defenses cracked—simply, quietly, slowly at first. A Christian friend of mine wrote a song that talked about God's love. That song penetrated me and described precisely what I needed. I began to see that God *did* accept me and cared about me even the way I was. I didn't have to shed one hundred pounds before God would say, "Karen, come into my family." Brick by brick, my wall of mistrust and bitterness began to crumble.

The interesting thing was that while I didn't need to slim down for God, after I gave my life to him I found he helped me do what, through all the years of struggle, I could never do for myself. After I became a Christian, God gave me a gift—self-control. It was not a magic prescription I swallowed like a diet pill, and presto—the pounds were gone. It was, rather, a slow, painful process: days and weeks and even years of saying "no" when I desperately wanted to say "yes."

Today I am two hundred pounds lighter. Some days I feel like the new creation I am in Christ. Other days I think of myself as the same unlovable, unacceptable Karen, and I worry about what people think of me. But I guess that just goes to show that God and I still have some projects we need to work on.

DRINKING MY WAY

Michael Hovart with Jim Long

I remember feeling isolated, even in a group; alone, even with people all around.

I often had the sensation I was fighting the crowd, like I was the only one trying to get into a room while everyone else was trying to get out. Other people were around but not really involved with me.

There was one group in school I always wanted to be part of. I thought that if I could just be friends with those guys, everything would be great. So I started drinking—because they did. It was just a part of being with them, but it became more than that. It became a habit.

During the summer between my junior and senior years, I moved away from home and into an apartment. I had no one to answer to and I could do whatever I wanted. So my place became the logical choice for parties. Things were shaping up for a great year. Yet somehow, I wasn't feeling all that great. I got what I thought I had wanted socially, but I didn't feel right about having it.

It was as if my apartment and my compromising were buying me what I wanted: acceptance. Yet I felt uneasy about the compromising. I wanted people to accept me as I was, not because I happened to have a convenient place for parties. My drinking became the focus of this uneasiness because that was my big area of compromise.

I soon discovered that it was not easy to stop. And even if I could have, I would have had to gamble my friendships, and I wasn't sure I wanted to risk that much just to break the habit.

These mixed feelings came to the surface at the first football game of the season. My friends had been notified to meet at my place about 6:30 P.M. They came with some other friends, bringing the beer and wine they had been drinking. Forty of us squeezed into my small apartment and

It was as if my apartment and my compromising were buying me what I wanted: acceptance.

continued drinking until about 7:15 when we left for the game, rowdy and drunk.

On the way to MacArthur High School, the opposing team's school, we stopped at Beverage King and bought some more beer, in quart bottles. By the time the game started at 8:00, I had downed a few quarts and was feeling bloated. I was also having difficulty focusing on things. Things were hazy, out of proportion.

I stood in the stands on the visitor side and squinted across the field. The home-team stands blurred into a panel of color. But there was a commotion, too. A few intoxicated trouble-makers from our school walked through the only entrance and promptly picked a fight with some guys from MacArthur. Before long, the fight erupted into a brawl with dozens of MacArthur students going after those few who had started the whole thing. I suddenly felt very conspicuous not being from MacArthur, standing on the visitor side, drunk and dizzy.

The whole opposite side of the field was beginning to look like one massive human wall—about 200 people—blocking the only

exit. And *they* were angry. Smaller fights were breaking out all around. Someone said the guys who started it all hopped the back fence.

I stood there watching all this, and in my alcohol-muddled brain, I was sure I'd be the next guy to get messed up. I felt too queasy to be heroic. I had that hopeless feeling you get when you are sure something is totally out of your control and all you can do is wait to see what will develop. Whether it made sense or not, I kept thinking I would not be in the situation if it weren't for my friends and the beer I had been guzzling earlier that evening.

Late that night, home alone, I started thinking through my big compromise problems, and it hit me just how wrong and pointless drinking seemed. I began to think breaking that habit might be worth the effort. Still, I was concerned about not losing face with my friends, so I manufactured a convenient excuse to use when someone offered me a beer, and I found the willpower to say no. "Well, I'm going out for wrestling" (which I was) "and I'm not supposed to drink" (which I wasn't).

If you aren't getting drunk yourself, there is nothing more annoying than a drunk person.

Then came the Toga Party, a la *Animal House*. The parents of one of the guys were out of town, so we put together one incredible bash. We printed invitations, charged a few bucks for admission, and required everyone to wear a toga to get in. There was a huge decorated cake and fifteen cases of beer. It was the major status event of the year. If you were invited to Steve's Toga Party, you were *in*.

But that night I just walked around watching my sheet-clad friends getting more and more drunk. And the thought hit me that it wasn't any fun to go to a party where everyone but me was drinking. In fact, I concluded, if you aren't getting drunk yourself, there is nothing more annoying than a drunk person. That was a new concept to me.

For the first time as a casual observer, I watched my friends smashed out of their minds. It was a ridiculous, almost eerie sensation. I left early that evening, realizing I had just attended the big party of my senior year and I hadn't even had a good time. It was as if I were a spectator at someone else's party.

That same feeling was confirmed a couple of weeks later at a friend's house. It was just a small party, a casual get-together. But I had that same spectator sensation—in the crowd, yet isolated: people all around, yet alone.

As I stood there with my hands empty, I felt conspicuous and awkward. I wanted to do something with my hands, so I grabbed a beer. But I had lost so much of my taste for alcohol over the past few weeks that I drank only about half of it. I stood for a while longer, alone, quiet, then I left. The half-empty can sat untouched in the beverage holder on the side panel of my car for weeks before I finally dumped it out.

I began to realize that I actually felt uncomfortable with the group I had tried so hard to be part of. I started avoiding the parties and being more honest about my reasons for not drinking. I had become a Christian when I was quite young, but my compromising had pushed God aside. When that happened, it was easy to get tangled up with the alcohol problem.

The Campus Life Guide

My hassle with alcohol was symptomatic of a deeper struggle.

I knew that drinking was not the true conflict; it was merely a surface battle. My hassle with alcohol was symptomatic of a deeper struggle—an internal conflict. But that habit had become a wedge driving me and God apart. It was when I was willing to walk back through the crowd, even if it meant being isolated and alone, that I found there are some things more important than the conditional "acceptance" they had to offer. And what was more surprising was that, as I let God control me, I found that anything could change with time, even the habit I knew I had to dump.

THE LOOK
OF LUST

Name Withheld

I remember vividly the night I first experienced real lust. In previous years I had drooled through *Playboy*, sneaked off to my uncle's room for a heart-thumping first look at hard-core pornography, and done my share of grappling and fumbling with my girlfriend's clothes. But my first willful commitment to lust occurred during a visit to upstate New York. I was alone, flipping through the city guide of what to do in Rochester, and I kept returning to one haunting photo of an exotic dancer, a former Miss Peach Bowl winner, the ad said. She looked fresh and inviting: the enchanting kind of Southern girl you see on television commercials for fried chicken—only this one had no clothes on.

Since I was a Christian, I instinctively ruled her show out of bounds for me. But as I settled down to watch an inane television show, her body kept looming before my mind with the simple question, "Why not?"

I began to think. Indeed, why not? To be an effective Christian, I had to experience all of life, right? Didn't Jesus himself hang around with prostitutes and sinners? I could go simply as an observer, "in the world but not of the world." Rationalizations leaped up to support my desires, and within ten minutes I hopped into the back seat of a taxi headed toward the seamy side of Rochester.

I got the driver to let me off a few blocks away, just for safety's sake, and I kept glancing over my shoulder in fear of seeing someone I knew. Or perhaps God would step in, extinguish my desires, and change my mind about the wisdom of the act. I even asked him about that, meekly. No answer.

I walked into the bar between acts and was then faced with the new experience of ordering a drink. Bolstered by my first fiery sips, which I tried to stretch out so as not to have to order another, I sat with my eyes glued to the stage.

Miss Peach Bowl was everything the ad had promised. With a

THE LOOK OF LUST

figure worthy of a Wonder Woman costume, she danced superbly and was something of an acrobat. She started fully clothed and teased us with slow removals of each sequined article of clothing. Toward the end, when she wore only a G-string; whooping men near the stage coaxed her to lean over and then they stuffed folded bills under the tiny swatch of cloth. She grinned invitingly: I stared in disbelief. In one final strobe-lit routine she cartwheeled nude across the stage.

The flush of excitement created by my first whiskey, drunk too fast in spite of myself, the eye-popping spectacle of a gorgeous woman baring all and jiggling in front of me, and the boisterous spirit of the all-male audience combined to overpower me. I walked out of the bar two hours later feeling strangely warmed, intensely excited, and surprised that nothing had actually happened to me.

*L*ust shares with sins like envy and pride the distinction of being invisible, slippery, hard to pin down. Was what happened that night a sin? I denied it to myself on the way home. To really rate as lust, I told myself, you must look on a woman so as to desire sexual intercourse with her. Isn't that what Jesus said? Whatever happened that night, I certainly couldn't recall desiring intercourse with Miss Peach Bowl. It was more private and distant than that. What happened, happened quickly, was gone, and left no scars. Or so I thought at the time.

Years have passed since that awakening in wintry Rochester, years spent never far from the presence of lust. The guilt caught up with me, and even that very evening, I was already praying slobbery prayers for forgiveness. For a while that guilt kept me out of live shows and limited my voyeurism to magazines and movies, but only for a while. For years I have fought unremitting guerrilla warfare.

Being the reflective sort, I have often mulled over the phenomenon of lust. It is unlike anything else in my experience. Most thrills—scary roller coasters, trips in airplanes, visits to waterfalls—lose a certain edge of excitement once I have experienced them and figured them out. I enjoy them, but after a few experiences they no longer hold such a powerful attraction.

Sex is completely different.

THE LOOK OF LUST

There is only so much to "figure out." Every person who endures high-school biology, let alone a sniggering sex-education class, knows the basic shapes, colors, and sizes of the sexual organs. Anyone who has been to an art museum knows about women's breasts. Anyone who has hauled down a gynecology book in a public library knows about genitalia. Somehow, no amount of knowledge reduces the appeal—the forces may, in fact, work together.

I learned quickly that lust, like physical sex, moves in only one direction. You cannot go back to a lower level and stay satisfied. You always want more. A magazine excites, a movie thrills, a live show really makes the blood run. But they do not satisfy; they only stir up.

*T*he night in Rochester was my first experience with adult lust, but by no means my last. Strip joints are too handy these days. The drug store down the street sells *Hustler*, *High Society*, *Jugs*, anythings you want. I have been to maybe fifteen truly pornographic movies. They make me very uncomfortable. Perhaps it is because it seems so deliberate and volitional to stand in line (always glancing around furtively), to pay out money, and to sit in the dark for an hour or two for the purpose of being aroused. The crowd is unlike any other crowd I mix with—they remind me I don't belong. And the movies, technically, aesthetically, and even erotically, are humdrum and boring. But still, when a local paper advertises one more *Emmanuelle* sequel, I drool.

I read numerous articles and books on temptation but found little help. If you boiled down all the verbiage and the ten-point lists of practical advice for coping with temptation, basically all they said was "Just stop doing it." That was easy to say. Practical "how-to" articles proved hopelessly inadequate, as if they said "Stop being hungry" to a starving man. Intellectually I might agree with their advice, but my glands would still secrete. What insight can change glands?

During those years I prayed to God hundreds of times for deliverance, but with no response. I began to view sex as another of God's mistakes, like tornadoes and earthquakes. In the final analysis, sex only caused me misery. Without it, I could conceive of becoming pure and god-

THE LOOK OF LUST

ly and all those other things the Bible exhorted me toward. With sex, any spiritual development seemed hopelessly unattainable.

I have described my downward slide in some detail not to feed your own interests and certainly not to nourish your own despair if you are floundering. I tell my struggles because they are real, but also to demonstrate that hope exists, that God can interrupt the terrible cycle of lust and despair. My primary message is one of hope, although until healing did occur, I had no optimism that it ever would.

But healing did begin, eventually, with a brief, simple book I picked up one day entitled *What I Believe*. It was written by a French Catholic author and novelist, Francois Mauriac. Included in the book was one chapter on purity that stood out from all the other Christian books I'd read on the subject.

After brazenly denying the most common reasons I have heard against succumbing to a life filled with lust, Mauriac concludes that there is only one reason to seek purity. It is the reason Christ proposed in the Beatitudes: "Blessed are the pure in heart, for they shall see God" (Matthew 5:8). Purity, says Mauriac, is the condition for a higher love—for a possession superior to all possessions: God himself.

Mauriac goes on to describe how most of our arguments for purity are negative arguments: Be pure, or you will feel guilty, or your marriage will fail, or you will be punished. But the Beatitudes clearly indicate a positive argument that fits neatly with the Bible's pattern in describing sins. Sins are not a list of petty irritations drawn up for the sake of a jealous God. Rather, they are a description of things that hinder our spiritual growth. We are the ones who suffer if we sin, by forfeiting the development of character and Christlikeness that would have resulted if we had not sinned.

The thought hit me like a bell rung in a dark, silent hall. So far, none of the scary, negative arguments against lust had succeeded in keeping me from it. Fear and guilt simply did not change my habits; they only added self-hatred to my problems. But here was a description of what I was missing by continuing to harbor lust: I was limiting my own intimacy with God. The love he offers is so transcendent and possessing that it requires our faculties to be purified and cleansed before we can possibly contain it.

I cannot tell you why a prayer that has been prayed for years is answered on the 1,000th request when God has met the first 999 with silence. But what I can tell you is that after reading that book, I prayed to God one more time, asking him not to cure me of my struggle, but instead to simply let me know he was there. And finally, God came through for me. The phrase may sound heretical, but to me, after so many years of failure, it felt as if he had suddenly decided to be there after a long absence. I prayed, hiding nothing (hide from God?), and he heard me.

I wish I could say that after that prayer, I never encountered another problem with lust. My struggles continued, and I slipped and fell several times. But something in me had changed, something that made it possible to say no to lust with much more regularity and certainty. And even more important, I gained a completely new perspective on purity. Purity was much more than a list of steamy situations for me to avoid. It was rather a positive effort to remove all hindrances to my spiritual growth, and to seek God's presence in my life. Though the war within me continues, I know God is there beside me. And that has made all the difference.

After reading my story, you can probably understand why I resist giving "practical advice" on lust. There are no ten easy steps to overcome temptation. At times the power of obsession overwhelms all reason or common sense. And yet, throughout my struggle, I did learn some valuable strategies, which I will add in hopes of preventing needless scars.

Recognize and name the problem. If it's lust, call it lust. You must admit your condition before it can be treated. Much of my earlier rationalizations were blatant attempts to shirk the name *lust*—I tried to redefine it.

Stop feeding lust. Killing fantasies is like trying not to think of a pink elephant, and there is no "magic bullet" solution to this problem. But cutting off desires through diversion, not dwelling on them when they begin, and trying to eliminate some of the mystery can help in the early stages of lust. The farther down the road you travel through books, magazines, films, and personal contacts, the more steps you must one day retrace.

Demythologize it. Sexual stimulations promise a lie. The objects of your fantasy are not going to go to bed with you—in fact, the photo sessions that create sexy photos are tiresome and mechanical, not at all erotic. Recognize that *Playboy* centerfolds are heavily retouched, and life is far different from what soft porn portrays it to be.

Confess its real price. I learned the ultimate price just in time, by watching a close friend who went beyond the point of no return and is today as miserable a person as I have ever met. In my case, lust demanded its tribute in the subtle and progressive loss of intimacy with the girl I loved and with God. My own self-respect was gradually deteriorating also.

Trace its history. Professional counselors have been helpful in pointing out the causes of my obsession that began in my sexually repressed childhood. For some people, lust comes from trying to win back the love of a distant parent or earning vengeance against a disappointing God or overcoming feelings of physical inadequacy by feeding myths. Friends and sometimes professional counselors can help you identify the cycle of lust by exploring its history with you.

Work on some positive addictions. Tennis, maybe, or scuba diving or hang-gliding. I've found that even video games preoccupy me for a time, especially when I am traveling. When I'm tempted to go to a sexually explicit movie, now I seek out a constructive film to occupy my evening. The obsession fades, at least temporarily.

Obsession arises from legitimate needs; follow them to their authentic source. I need God. I need a father. I need female friendship. I need to be hugged. I need to be loved, and to love. I need to feel worthwhile, attractive to someone. Those are my real needs, not the three-minute rush of voyeurism inside a twenty-five-cent booth. Let these real needs be met when the obsession arises, and the sexually based substitute may lose its grip.

Photo by Bob Combs

SECTION 6

FAMILY PROBLEMS

PROBLEMS

Jay Kesler

D o you know what it's like to lie in bed at night, listening to your parents fight? Have you lived with the gnawing worry that your parents were going to split up? It's a terrible feeling. You are no longer able to put any trust in things you once considered secure. It can make you feel hopeless and lost like nothing else. Why? Because nobody—not your friends, not your teachers, not your brothers or sisters—has the power to affect you like your parents.

Chances are, you aren't constantly paranoid about this. Though everything may not be perfect in your home, you probably have no serious doubts that things will hold together, even if your parents do fight.

But when your parents fight, the problems are all you can think about. Food is tasteless when you eat meals with a family that's feuding. Sleep is disturbed when you wake to the sound of loud voices. Peace of mind is hard to find when you're caught in the middle of a fight between two people you love in a deep way. What can you do?

A big part of the turmoil you're feeling has to do with your perspective. You're so close to the action that it's hard to separate yourself from it. It's as if you're playing a bit-part in a play in which your parents are the main characters. You might see your parents differently if you step out of the play and into the theater wings, where you can watch your parents as actors on the stage.

Let's say I go to see a production of *Hamlet*. As the play progresses, I get more and more caught up in the conflict. When I see the last scene, in which everyone gets killed, I can't stand it any longer; I leap up on the stage and try to throw myself between the actors. Or maybe I'm able to sit tight, but when I leave the theater I'm so worked up that I grab a knife and stab a few people, too. You would say I was making an inappropriate and bad response to the play. The best way to respond to *Hamlet* is to sit and watch the play and leave the theater thinking about it.

Yet if your parents are having trouble, your first reaction is to get involved in the fight. You want to leap up onstage and throw yourself between them. But it won't help anyone, because you're too minor a character. At this point some of the other major characters, such as clergymen, counselors, or relatives, need to come onstage and help their friends. But you can't.

Your second reaction is to go out and, inflamed by what's happened at home, to start acting with hostility, like your parents,

and to start hurting your friends. Or maybe you'll even take out some of your frustrations on yourself. But obviously that won't do any good either.

The best plan is to sit tight and stay out of things. It's rough, because you can't leave the theater—the emotions onstage really get to you. If you realize that you only have to live with this thing for a few more years, you may be able to grit your teeth and learn from it. The lessons will be invaluable for your future.

Of course, there is a way you can help. You can express your feelings and clear the air between you and your parents. Perhaps you can find a good time to sit down with them—when they're not fighting—and tell them how it's affecting you. Choose a time and place where it's quiet—dinner time, just before bed, Saturday morning—and be honest with them. You might be able to help your parents realize how serious their fighting is. But you can't solve their problems for them. If you try, you may get crushed in the middle of forces you're not strong enough to master. You should carry your end as well as possible—try not to mouth off, try to understand their problems, try to be pleasant. But you're not a family counselor. You can't sit them down and say, "Come on, Dad, we've got to straighten things out." Good or bad, whenever your parents look at you, they remember when you wore diapers. They can't imagine any smart advice coming out of you.

So generally you aren't going to single-handedly straighten out your family's problems. The most important thing is to keep your own head screwed on straight. But with all your emotions churning, how can you do that? It isn't easy. You may find these days to be the most emotionally trying times of your entire life. But survival is possible. Here are some general principles I'd suggest:

Never take sides. That won't be simple, because in any situation it will appear to you that one side is right and the other wrong. But when you get very far into a fight, you nearly always discover two sides to the story.

Suppose your dad comes home from work and seems quite irritable. Your mother says something, he overreacts, and it develops into a fight. At first you might feel protective of your mother and think, "Dad has no right to jump on her that way." But there may be a number of hidden factors you don't know about. For one thing, you don't know the kind of pressure your dad has been facing all day. He may be watching younger friends get laid off, or he may be worried about losing his job at forty years old. All of that may be involved in his being irritated at home.

"Well," you say, "it's not my mom's fault." But that isn't how a married couple looks at problems. If he's under that kind of pressure you mother ought to be helping him cope. Maybe she's not holding up her end. And maybe she's coping with pressures you don't understand.

Or there might be other factors, some apparent to you and some not. Perhaps they're having sexual problems. How are you going to know about that? There are too many possibilities for you to even think about taking sides intelligently. Even if you could, taking sides wouldn't help. Family problems will not be corrected if you go around trying to determine who's to blame and who isn't. You won't help anything. The blamed party feels guilty or angry, and the blameless party feels self-righ-

The Campus Life Guide

teous. To find a solution, you must have determined action by both parties.

Accept your parents, weaknesses and all. You can't do that if you believe in the prevalent American myth of the well-rounded person. There simply aren't any well-rounded people. Everybody has a bad side, a weak side. Everyone has needs, and that's why working together is such an important aspect of Christianity. We complement each other. If there were well-rounded people, they wouldn't need complementing.

So when looking at your parents, don't go looking for their faults. Look for their strengths. One person may have an excellent ability to love and accept, while another person's abilities lie in organization. Believe me, they're both essential; one isn't *better* than the other.

Be realistic. Remember that all families go through cycles. There are times when your parents are under more pressure than at other times. Don't freak out because one week is bad. Things sometimes get bad in the normal course of events, but they also get better.

Don't compare. It doesn't help comparing your own family with others. You may think a certain girl's dad is really nice when you're there, and you may wish your own father were like that. But you can't compare. You see her dad only in a good light—he's not going to spout off while you're around. He's in a totally different role with you—for instance, he's not in charge of disciplining you. So naturally, he comes off a little better.

Families are different from one another. How your parents act toward each other partially depends on their backgrounds. Certain ethnic groups tend to express themselves more. Maybe you're from an Italian family, and your parents argue loudly, yet without hostile feelings. You go to high school with a lot of kids from English or Scandinavian backgrounds, and you wish like crazy for the peace and quiet you find in their homes. But keep in mind that their homes aren't necessarily better just because they express themselves differently. Maybe that calmness is covering a feud. A silent feud is worse than an argument any day.

So don't just watch the arguments; watch for the kissing, the loving and forgiving. If your dad loses his temper and yells at your mom, but the next thing you know they're cooing and cuddling, and you're the fifth of eight kids—relax. It's just their style to yell. And if you don't see overt signs of affection between you parents, it's not necessarily because they don't love each other. People have different styles of expressing love. Some people come from homes where love isn't expressed by talking or touching. It's expressed by duty, like in the musical *Fiddler on the Roof:* "Whaddya mean, do I love you? I wash your socks, milk the cow, have your children. Of course I love you."

I suppose the most common reaction you have to problems between your parents is anxiety. Your parents are fighting and it gets to you. You lie awake at night listening to them fight, and a cold shadow creeps over your life; everything that means warmth and security is falling apart. You're sinking.

That helpless feeling is something you can't fight. Fighting it directly is like fighting quicksand; you only wear yourself out as you sink deeper and deeper into it. It can really hurt you. It can make you paranoid and afraid. It can make you talk too much or clam up with your problems.

It can also teach you some extremely valuable lessons. When you think of how desperate and panicked those feelings of helplessness can be, think about your parents' feeling exactly the same way. They probably do. They are already straining with anxiety over growing old. Most people are very frightened of middle age and old age. They realize how economically vulnerable they are; at that age, what does happen if you lose your job? And then the frustrations of marriage, which they probably thought would be their dream-come-true, add to that. They are going to be living with those problems the rest of their lives, while you just have to survive two or three more years.

You're probably just one of a family of anxiety-ridden people. Realize that, and you'll be able to empathize with your parents. You will be able to talk to them better, understand them better. You will even find yourself feeling sorry for them, which in small doses isn't all bad.

Those feelings of anxiety can do even more for you; they may drive you to the rock bottom source of security. I like to think of life as a system of bonuses. The only thing that absolutely cannot fail you, no matter how rotten you are or how rotten the world is, is God's love. Everything beyond that is a wonderful bonus. Maybe you have one friend in the world. That may seem bad, but actually that one friend is a precious bonus. You weren't guaranteed any. Maybe you're doing well in school, and you're going to get the education you need and get a good job. That's a bonus, too. Maybe you have a steady temperament, and your emotions don't soar up and down every five minutes. That's a bonus. All the things in life are bonuses, and they ought to be thought of that way. The only thing that isn't a bonus, that is guaranteed, is "God loves you."

Everything else may be stripped away. Friends can be stripped away. The security of a home can be stripped away. Warmth and food can be taken away. Your own mental stability can go out the window. The only genuinely sure thing is God. "He will keep in perfect peace all those who trust in him, whose thoughts turn often to the Lord" (Isa. 26:3). We like to live believing in the stability of other things. But ultimately we need to push our roots down deep enough to realize this is our only true stability.

Instead of letting anxiety about your parents drive you into a frenzy, you should allow it to drive you deeper into God's grace. Only when you've done this, can you really cure anxiety, and the love you get at home will be truly a bonus to you, an *extra for which you're thankful.*

I ncreasingly, problems between parents are going into court and ending in divorce. Thousands of kids must cope with their parents' separation or divorce every year. Maybe you're one of them. Maybe you're going to be one of them. Or maybe you just worry that you're going to be one of them.

It may help to know that it's not the end of the world. It can be very, very difficult, but even at its worst, it is the kind of thing you can live through.

Most of the principles for surviving a divorce are the same as those for surviving parental fights. You are going to want to take sides, and in some cases your parents will try to drag you into it. It's only natural for you to feel that one person is right and the other wrong, whether you have an accurate picture or not.

I would caution you, however, to maintain as much objectivity as possible, particularly by loving *both* parents. If you show a spirit of forgiveness, it'll be easier for your parents to do the same.

Often, it becomes tedious living with one parent. That parent has to be all things to you, while the other parent only comes in once in a while and treats you to nice things. Try consciously not to glamorize the parent you don't live with, and don't verbally compare them. There are enough wounds between them without flicking off scabs.

You may feel—many do—that the divorce or separation was your fault. Even if your parents point at you, fight over you, or blame you for their troubles, it is highly unlikely that you are the cause. Psychologists and marriage counselors have observed again and again that the problems that led your parents to separate or divorce began long before you arrived on the scene, perhaps even during your parents' childhood. So whatever you do, don't blame or punish yourself for what has happened.

W hen there are constant problems in the family, you should become more aware of yourself, especially when living with only one parent. Find some adult you can trust, someone who will understand, someone without any ulterior motives. Adults are usually much more open to being a friend to you than you'd think at first; in fact, most would welcome it.

Older brothers and sisters can also be a very important bridge. They may have far deeper understanding of the problems that led to the divorce; talking to them can help. If you're an older brother or sister, I think you ought to be particularly sensitive to ways you can heal the pain in your younger brothers and sisters. Just talking things out can be tremendously healing.

D on't forget to consider professional counseling if you're not getting the help and support you need from other people. Licensed counselors or therapists are trained to help you identify and work out the problems you're facing with your parents.

If your parents are having problems, make sure you're not contributing to them. You can create friction by making demands that strain your parents' finances (a lot of fighting is over money). Or you put a strain on your mother's time when you know she's busy. If you want a peaceful home, you must help create it. That may require giving up some of the things you want

The Campus Life Guide

in order to preserve peace. The unwillingness to give anything up for another's good is one of the biggest problems of any marriage—and you're a part of the equation.

You know how an oyster makes a pearl? A pearl begins with some kind of irritation coming into the life of the oyster—a grain of sand, or a piece of shell. Instead of trying to expel the irritation, which an oyster can't do anyway, the oyster surrounds it with its own body fluids and gradually encases it with a smooth coating, eventually turning it into a beautiful pearl.

Extreme problems, like those with troubled parents, can have the same effect on you. If you surround them with love and understanding, gaining personal insight for your own future, you will end up with something infinitely valuable. You will develop a personal character that will help you cope with life's problems, able to help yourself and others. It may be that God has a future need for a great number of people who know how it feels to be a child from a troubled home.

SEPARATE WAYS

Becki Reeves as told to S. Rickly Christian

On the hope chest beside me sits a black and white picture of a man I hardly know: my father. He was barely twenty the year he posed for the camera in his crisp Air Force uniform—not yet married, slim, proud shoulders, chiseled jaw, and sandy blond hair.

But he has changed over the last twenty-six years. It is as if he stood rigid in an open field as it started to snow. Slowly, the flakes began to blanket him until his image was covered and rounded off—altered beyond recognition.

I often wondered, after my father left home, whether I could ever steel myself enough to draw a picture of him as I had done for other family members. But sitting now with my drawing pencil in hand and sketch pad propped in my lap, I find the task of transferring highlights from the military portrait onto paper relatively easy. But I can do it without crying only because the man in the tarnished gold frame looks nothing like the man I grew up calling, *"father"*—

heavy jowl, balding, fat, and very lonely.

"Father," I thought to myself as I drew, *"I wish you knew how I feel some nights when I cry myself to sleep because I was never able to call you 'Daddy.' You always wanted to be called 'Father,' and that seemed so stiff."*

My father once admitted to Mom that he had built a wall around himself, and that if anybody came too close it would shake the bricks. He never made close friends, because he never seemed to want them. It's not that he couldn't relate to other people; as a pilot for United Airlines he had to. But his relationships were on a very unemotional level. He could talk easily if conversation were limited to aviation and planes, and he did well at bowling, where interaction was at a minimum. But beyond that he squirmed.

He had a way of distancing himself—similar to the way he responded when flying through

Mom and Dad's real problem was that they were two completely different people.

a thunderstorm with his plane bouncing up and down, thousands of feet in the air. The passengers would be scared to death. But my father would pick up the mike and, in his cold, static official drawl, calmly announce that passengers should fasten their seat belts due to minor turbulence.

He never understood why others could be so racked with emotion that they would cry, laugh, or scream at each other. When my parents had conflicts, my father would either leave the room and drive away or distance himself mentally. He never showed his feelings or yelled back.

"Scream at me, I don't care!" Mom would shout. "Do something, say anything. Just tell me how you're feeling!" But my father never responded, and Mom finally gave up trying to force him.

It's not that they fought frequently. My father was too withdrawn and unfeeling for that. Their real problem was that they were two completely different people. Mom never wanted much from my father but to be loved by him. She focused on the family and had so much love to give. He seemed to have none. She was the one that always drove us kids places even when it was inconvenient for her; who always went out of her way to ensure the family's needs were met. He never seemed to realize we had needs.

Mom wanted holidays to be special family times. But they never were. To my father, any holiday was as unimportant and uneventful as a dog-day afternoon in the middle of summer. Even Christmas, which was also their wedding anniversary, was just another day of the week to him. Mom always bought the Christmas presents and signed them, "Love, Mom and Dad." But he generally sat on the sidelines as the rest of the family laughed together and opened presents. Then he'd take off and drive all day, up and down empty farm roads and deserted highways. To me it seemed he resented Christmas because it was the day he married Mom.

If he remained home for lesser holidays and birthdays, it was only out of obligation. And even then, he sometimes spent the time alone, digging in the garden on our five-acres in the country. He never wanted us kids to help

> *"I can't live with your mother anymore. It's just not working out," he began.*

with the gardening because he seemed to think we messed things up. I tried to help him once, but pulled up a carrot instead of a weed. He didn't say much, but glared at me with eyes as cold as the unturned October turf.

"Father, I wish you understood I'm missing part of myself because of your rejection of me. For all the years we shared the same house, your eyes were never warm."

A couple of years ago, my father went off camping by himself for an entire month; nobody knew where he was. He returned home for my sixteenth birthday and said he wanted to take me and my two brothers out for my birthday dinner. But he didn't want Mom along.

At the restaurant, we hardly talked. What little conversation we had was mostly small talk. Our fish came, we ate, then the waitress came with the check. But before we slid out of the red vinyl booth, my father said there was something he had to say.

"I can't live with your mother anymore. It's just not working out," he began.

I wanted to cry, to scream, even to slap him. But I've always been good at hiding my emotions from him, so I just sat there, staring hard at the shadowy images flickering from the dim candle in the center of the table. He said he wanted to leave, that he had to leave. But suddenly it felt like he'd left years ago; like I never had a father. Anger and bitterness surged within me, and I felt sick to my stomach. I didn't hear anything else my father said.

"Take me home. I want to go home now," I said, interrupting whatever he was saying. I slid out and walked to the door, hoping it was all a dream. But once outside, the stiff September wind whipped my senses wide awake. And the hurt was still there.

As we drove down the long country roads, nobody talking, I knew I couldn't go home just yet. Mom would be crying because my birthday was ruined and she was losing a husband. And my father would just sit by himself in the living room, his cold empty eyes seeing nothing, reflecting his quiet despair. Besides, tonight was Sunday, and others would expect me at

I didn't see it as my parents' problem.
I saw it as mine.

church. I was almost a fixture there—as much a part of the church as the sanctuary pews.

"Please take me to church," I said without looking at him. The headlights of my father's rusty Cutlass carved a swath of brightness in the black night, illuminating the scraggly oaks which bordered the road like an impenetrable fence.

Hunched low in my seat, I glanced at my father. His baggy, mustached face glowed slightly green from the dashboard lights before he turned away to check the sideview mirror.

When he pulled into the church's parking lot, I scrambled out of the car, slammed the door, and walked toward the lighted building. Only when I knew the car was gone did I cry. But I was a leader of the youth group, so I fought to choke back the tears. I had always been the steady one in the group—the Christian that others looked to for help with their problems. They wouldn't understand if I fell apart over my parents' problem, I thought. Trouble was, I didn't see it as my parents' problem. I saw it as mine. The rejection, hurt, and guilt that overwhelmed me seemed too personal for the problem to be anybody's but mine.

I somehow managed to regain control and make it through the church service without breaking down. Then I caught a ride home with a friend.

I went straight to my room, but as soon as I crawled into bed my father walked in. He stepped to the side of my bed and knelt beside me.

"Becki, I'm sorry about tonight. But this . . ." he began, stumbling over the words, "this is something I have to do. Things just aren't good with your mother and me. They've never been good."

Why was he assuaging his guilt by telling me these things? He didn't have to explain anything. I stared past him to the bulletin board on my far wall, but couldn't say a word. I knew if I tried, my voice would quaver, and I would burst into racking sobs. I just wanted him to leave.

"But I want you to know that no matter what happens, I . . . I love you," he said quickly, trying to hide his uneasiness. Then he turned and was gone, leaving me clinging to my pillow in tears. It was the first time he had ever said he loved me.

If he really loved me, then why did he leave?

"Father, I wish you knew how hard it was for me to hide my emotions from you. But you seemed to disdain Mom for showing hers, and I don't want to be rejected for the same reason," I reflect as I survey my progress on the drawing of my father. "What happened to you so long ago that prevents you from laughing, joking around, and being a bit crazy? Father, you always looked so dreadfully lonely."

Two days later, he left. I watched from my upstairs bedroom window as he packed a small black and white television and a few personal belongings into his trailer and pulled out of our lives. My face was pressed to the glass as the car eased down our rutted, unpaved driveway and disappeared beyond the far bank of trees, raising a cloud of dust behind.

I saw him only periodically after he moved out and rented a small house a few miles away.

"How long's it been?" he asked me the first time I stopped by.

"Three months."

"No kidding. Has it been that long?" He shrugged it off, saying something about being so busy. Then he showed me his place: lawn chairs as living room furniture, television set on a crate, cheap foam pads thrown down as a mattress, no dresser. "It's not much, but it's livable," he said.

It hurt to see him living like that, though I tried not to care. After all, I thought, it serves him right for having deserted the family. It was like he had dropped a bomb on us, then didn't hang around to see the damage. Mom was shattered. There weren't many nights when she didn't cry herself to sleep. My brothers tried their best to cope, but their hurt was reflected in their eyes. And I found it hard to fight the rush of bitter feelings toward my father that engulfed me. If he really loved me, then why did he leave?

And how was I supposed to act at church where my father had served as treasurer? To outsiders, the Reeves family was good and solid—absolutely the last family anybody would have expected to fall apart. In the eyes of those in the youth group, I was level-headed and emotionally calm. What would they think if they knew I was just hiding

I told God I felt totally crushed by my parent's situation.

my feelings behind a papier-maché smile that was beginning to crack?

I wanted to talk to somebody, but who was there? I generally felt okay at school where there were distractions to keep my mind busy. But what about after eighth period when the friends and distractions were gone? Where could I turn for help during the lonely hours before I could fall asleep at night?

In some ways I was afraid to talk to anybody about my problems, because I was uncertain what they would think. To others, Becki Reeves just didn't seem to have problems. But my emotional facade was beginning to fall apart.

I finally turned to the youth pastor at church. Sitting in his booklined office, I closed my eyes and took a deep breath before I could manage to find any words at all. It was a groping effort to be honest, but I stumbled along for two hours. When I finished, I expected to get a sermon in return. But he didn't preach. He didn't say I would feel better if I just had more faith. Rather, he explained that it's normal for Christians to feel crummy at times—to feel their

world is caving in. But instead of denying those feelings exist, he said it was important that I admit they were there and work through them with God's help.

That night as I lay in bed, staring at the white tiles of my ceiling, I thought about what my youth pastor had said. *With God's help.* That certainly made sense. So I struggled to express my feelings of bitterness and anger, of hurt and confusion. I told God I felt totally crushed by my parents' situation, and that I didn't think I loved my father. I told him it didn't make sense—but there was something inside me that craved for a daddy's shoulder to cry on, for a daddy's strong arms to hold me and give me a sense of security and confidence. Without that, I told God, I didn't feel like a whole person.

It seemed amazing, but God in a sense became that father I could turn to. I'm not saying that the going was easy from then on, or that my problems and feelings disappeared overnight. It still hurt. But I felt God somehow understood. And by opening my heart to him, I gained a sense of security and confidence to face my problems.

I began to admit that he might never come back.

"Father, I wish you knew I pray for you at night. Though I want you back home, I sometimes feel that same deep pain inside that comes when I don't think you really love me."

After my father had been away nearly two years, I began to admit that he might never come back. Technically, the door was still open because the divorce papers had never been finalized. But he didn't come around much. Maybe he thought we didn't love him. Maybe he thought we didn't want him back. I didn't know. And I would never have asked.

But I decided one day I wouldn't wait for him to make the first move. I would call him. I would do something special for him.

I had drawn pictures of other members of my family. But I have never drawn my father. So that's why I sit now with a sketch pad propped on my lap, drawing a picture of a man I hardly know. . . .

"Father, I wish you knew how scared I am to stick out my neck like this, to love you first. I'm scared you might reject what little I have to give. Though I am a young woman now, almost grown, I still have the ceramic heart of a little girl. So, Father, if I call you 'Daddy' and hug you when I give you this picture, please hug me back."

NO
MIRACLES

Brad Ferguson as told to S. Rickly Christian

My mom and dad were drunks. That pretty much describes them.

I don't know much about dad, other than the bits and pieces Mom revealed over the years. She met him at work on the rebound from her first marriage. He had a serious drinking problem and she was a divorcee. They were both lonely and conveniently fell in love. Mom, who wasn't drinking much then, tried to dry him out after their marriage, but he died when I was five. On his death certificate, the cause of death is listed as alcoholism.

As I grew up, I often wondered why Mom never dated or got married again. I asked her about it late one Sunday night when we were home alone. Sipping a glass of wine as she cleaned the kitchen, she pretended she didn't hear the question. So I asked again. She shrugged, and without turning around, mumbled something about that being the way life is sometimes. But I guessed the real reason was that she didn't want to risk being hurt a third time. Two marriages were enough.

Mom was an able provider on her own, but she was so overprotective she embarrassed me. Until sixth grade, I had a regular baby-sitter. She insisted I wear a crew cut when everybody else had long hair. And Mom always made me ride my bike on the sidewalk. Kids at my junior high school never forgot such things. Nor did I. "Hey Ferguson," the guys yelled as I pedaled to school one day, "your mom will probably make you drive your car on the sidewalk, too!"

I was always the brunt of other kids' jokes. And Mom was the cause. She just couldn't bear to let me grow up. So she clutched me as tight and as long as she possibly could, and I resented it.

Not only did her stringent attitude affect me, but it also took its toll on her. I didn't know why, but Mom always seemed as if she were

NO MIRACLES

under pressure. I think she was afraid to relax. It was as if she feared all her anxieties would overwhelm her during an unguarded moment. So she kept herself busy, her glass filled, and tried to out-distance whatever fears haunted her.

Weekdays, I'd hear her alarm rattle at 6 A.M. Her routine never changed. She'd scan the morning paper, feed the dog, shower, eat, fix sack lunches for herself and me, maybe iron a blouse, drop me off at school, then head to the Buick dealership in San Diego where she worked.

When she returned home about 6:30 each night, she was usually cranky. She'd yell something about the house being a mess, then pour herself a glass of wine and start to clean or cook.

Drinking seemed to calm her. But by the time I was in high school, she needed more than a nightly glass to unwind. She needed a bottle or two.

Because of that, driving with Mom was always a terror. I remember the time early in my sophomore year when we were together in the car. I didn't have my license yet. She was weaving badly, and I kept asking her to pull over and stop. Finally she ran a stop sign and broadsided another car. When the police arrived, Mom saluted playfully. " 'Scuse me, Ocifer," she said in a drunken slur before she was handcuffed and taken to jail. I got a ride home in the squad car.

At my urging, Mom enrolled in a local Alcoholics Anonymous program, but she quit after the second meeting, saying it made her feel like a common drunk. Maybe they just forced her to admit she had a problem, and she wasn't ready to do that yet.

I thought relatives might be able to help. But they seemed as determined as Mom was to ignore the extent of her problem. I didn't know what else I could do.

I hated Mom for drinking. But I couldn't stop caring. At night, during television commercials, I watched her from the corner of my eyes as she slaved in the kitchen, a drink in her hand. She always looked so lonely, so dreadfully lonely.

Since I'd become a Christian back in junior high, I half-expected a miracle would be included in the deal—a miracle to relieve Mom's loneliness and remove her dependence on alcohol. But that didn't happen. And it

NO MIRACLES

seemed that God was failing me, because Mom only got worse.

One night I arrived home late from school. The lights were on, and Mom was slouched in her favorite living-room chair nursing a drink. An empty wine bottle was lying on the floor beside her. I knew she was already loaded and I'd have to carry her to bed and fix my own dinner.

"You drunk!" I yelled and slammed the front door. "Don't you know you're killing yourself? That you're doing just what you said Dad did? You're no good to anybody like this!" I shouted from across the room.

She just sat there and tried to focus on her glass as she raised it to her lips.

"Doan talk so loud, shweedart," she said, a crooked grin crossing her face as she took another sip.

Suddenly I could take no more. I threw my school books against the couch and stomped to the bookshelf.

"I can't stand you!" I cried, dumping a set of encyclopedias on the floor. I grabbed at books as fast as I could and boomed them against the wall. "I can't stand you!" I shouted again, the tears flooding my eyes. "You don't think about me. You don't think about anybody. You're killing yourself and don't even care!" When I ran out of books, I overturned a table, dumped a chair, then stormed down the hall into the bathroom. I slammed the door behind me, and began hysterically beating a hole in the plaster wall with my fist.

The following day after school, I stayed at the beach until sunset. Instead of going home, I called Mark, a good friend from church, and asked if I could spend the night at his house. We'd gotten to be friends at church where he taught the high-school class. And he'd always been willing to help when things got especially bad.

When I arrived, Mark was shooting pool. I joined him for a few games of eight-ball but couldn't concentrate. I kept thinking about Mom being home alone.

"Maybe I should call to check up," I said. "She doesn't even know where I am."

"Go ahead, I'll wait," he said.

As the phone rang, I tried to think of what I'd say when Mom answered. *Maybe I should try a new approach, I thought. Blowing up hadn't seemed to work.*

For the first time since I'd become a Christian, I tried to

NO MIRACLES

imagine what Jesus' reaction would be to her. I found it hard to imagine him calling Mom a drunk. Though he could never condone her drunkenness, he'd most certainly overwhelm her with love and forgiveness—something I had not done.

After ten rings, Mom answered the phone.

"Hi," I said.

"Brad?"

"Yeah, I just called to say I'm over at Mark's, and that . . . well, I love you, Mom." The words sounded strange in my mouth, and I waited for her response. But all I could hear was her heavy breathing. She was probably too far gone to understand.

D uring the remainder of my sophomore year Mom continued to drink heavily. The months until June were a blur of drunk-driving charges, trips to the county detoxification center, and long, lonely nights that she spent with a glass in her hand.

One summer night I was able to get through to her by approaching her early in the eve-ning.

"Please, Mom," I said, looking her straight in the eye, "please don't get drunk tonight."

She looked at me for a long moment, then set down her glass.

"I just want to get to know you as a person for once. And I can't do that when you're drunk."

She didn't go near the bottle the rest of the night. After dinner we had a chance to talk—for the first time in years.

We sat on the floor in the living room and talked for several hours about normal things—Mom's job, future goals, my girlfriend, the garden out back. It wasn't easy for her to sit still without a drink; I could see the struggle in her eyes and the almost imperceptible shake of her hands. To help her, I kept filling her glass with orange juice, water . . . anything but alcohol.

Late in the evening, the conversation turned to God, and I had a chance to talk to Mom about my beliefs.

"Mom," I said, "you've tried to find satisfaction outside of God. There isn't any. In fact, your drinking is robbing you of

NO MIRACLES

the abundant life God wants for you.*

"And don't you see you're drinking yourself to death? Just like Dad."

Mom looked down at the rug and started to cry softly.

"Brad," she said, dabbing at her tears, "I need help."

I knew I couldn't provide the help she needed. So I leaned over, clasped her hands in mine and prayed for her out loud. I asked God to be close to her and free her from the bondage she experienced as an alcoholic.

"Please, Lord," I concluded. "Mom needs your help."

Maybe I should have prayed for God to help *me*, because two weeks later I blew up again. Mom still refused to attend Alcoholics Anonymous meetings. She could have received support there from people who understood her problem. Without that, she just wound up drunk night after night. And I couldn't stand it any longer. So I moved out of my house and into a home rented by several Christian friends.

_____
*John 10:10

One day in early August, I called Mom to check how she was. But there was no answer. It was unusual for her not to be home in the evening, so I called a couple of neighbors to see if they knew her whereabouts. None did. So I called the Buick dealership where she worked.

"Your mother was rushed to the hospital two days ago," a salesman said.

"She what?"

"She's at Mercy Hospital. They're running tests."

I figured Mom's problems were alcohol-related—cirrhosis of the liver or something like that. But when I got to the hospital, the doctor was at the nurse's station and drew me aside.

"Brad," he said, "your mother has cancer."

"Cancer?"

"We performed a biopsy yesterday. Her whole body is infested—the back side of her brain, both lungs, spinal cord, her kidney, liver—about every major organ."

"How long, Doctor?" I asked, trying to verbalize a question that seemed impossible to ask.

"It could be tomorrow. It could be a month. But probably just a week or two."

NO MIRACLES

"Did it have anything to do with her drinking?"

"No."

"Where is she now?" I asked.

"Room 216. Brad, I'm sorry. But there's nothing we could do. It's something she's had for at least ten years."

I nodded slowly, then turned down the hall. When I reached the room and stepped inside, Mom was lying on the bed, babbling incoherently.

As I stood above her, hoping for some glint of recognition in her eyes, a lot of things began to make sense. Back when I was in the fourth grade, Mom had had an operation to remove a cancerous lump in her breast. When she returned home afterwards, I assumed everything was okay. And she never said anything. I thought of all the brown plastic containers in our medicine cabinet. She'd been taking the pills for as long as I could recall—pills she'd said were for high blood pressure. But I never knew for sure.

My mind was flooded as I stood there. Perhaps Mom knew all along she had cancer but refused treatment. Maybe she thought drinking was a way to help her cope.

But that's something I'll never know because she died two weeks later. And whenever I visited her before her death, she was incoherent.

I wish I'd had a chance to tell Mom goodbye, to thank her for all those 6 A.M. mornings, for the thousands of lunches, and for all the other things she did for me over the years. I wish I could have held her and asked her forgiveness for my insensitivity, for my Christian love that seemed to flip-flop to resentment and hate about every other day.

It's a slow process, but God is helping me deal with those feelings. I still don't think Mom's drinking was right, and I wish she'd told me about her illness, but I do recall numerous times when I should have been more sensitive. I believe God's forgiven me for those times. And I also know I can turn to him for support whenever I can't cope.

HOUSEFUL OF STRANGERS

Philip Yancey

"This whole family disgusts me!" April scraped her chair across the oak floor. "There are pieces of your lives scattered all over the country." She looked at Mother and Dad. "Lovers, children, whole parts of families which you've cut off as if they don't exist."

Dad put down his fork and started to speak, but April wouldn't let him. "Instead we're stuck with this *let's-pretend* family. We sit around a plastic tablecloth like Barbie Dolls, pretending to get along. It disgusts me. I hate all of you, and I refuse to use words like father and brother in a house full of strangers!"

Then April wadded up her napkin, threw it in the center of the mashed potatoes, and stomped outdoors.

No one spoke for at least five minutes. Dad was furious, I could tell. His head was down, and I could see the vein in his bald spot pumping a rhythm. He chewed his food fast and nervously.

Mother busied herself passing seconds to Dad and me, and after a while she picked up a glass vial and said matter-of-factly, "April didn't take her epilepsy pill again."

No one else spoke during the meal. We clinked our silverware against the dishes, chewed the food, and stared straight ahead. Mother served ice cream in silence and we ate it in silence. April had succeeded in destroying another meal.

I wandered to my room and put on a Journey album. Mother and Dad usually objected, especially at the volume I was playing it, but I knew they wouldn't say anything this time. Even they would understand the need to shatter the silence. I lay on the bed and stared at the posters on the wall.

The experiment wasn't working. Outside my window were the red hills of Santa Fe, dotted with pinon pine. They seemed to glow in the afternoon sun like an infrared photograph. We had come to this desolate place in one last effort to hold the "family" together.

121

NO PROBLEM

NO PROBLEM

33

Photo by Verne

HOUSEFUL OF STRANGERS

April was right. There was no glue in our "family," just four people in New Mexico. My mother had died when I was nine, and Dad had married Mother, April's mother, who had been married twice before. Four of her kids were living with their fathers. April, the fifth, was stuck with Mother because her father didn't want her.

Dad took a cut in pay and moved to New Mexico, for April's sake. Perhaps a change in scenery would change April, he thought. She had been freaking out in New Jersey. With all my cousins and grandparents and aunts around, she had felt trapped. So she'd regularly stay out all night and come home stoned.

Mother would talk to me about April. It was weird, having an adult come to my room crying and asking for help. She would tell the same stories over and over: "April just couldn't accept it when her father left us. She just can't face rejection." April blamed Mother for poisoning April's father against her.

Mother would tell me the stories and plead with me to help. "Help me love April, James!" she would beg. How many dozen times had I heard her say that? I kept wanting to say,

"Mother, what you mean is 'Help me *change* April.' " But I didn't want to hurt her.

I had tried to talk seriously with April. No response. We'd lived together six years, shared the same bathroom, eaten meals together. But she wasn't really my sister, and she stayed aloof enough to remind me of that.

When she came home that night, after the dinner table explosion, I went to her room. She was draped over a beanbag chair, watching a movie on her four-inch Sony portable. April was almost beautiful, but also wild-looking. She was wearing the short-shorts that made Mother so mad and a T-shirt with a suggestive slogan printed on it. She glanced up but did not greet me. Her eyes had the look of hatred usually reserved for her mother and my grandmother.

I watched the movie for a few minutes, leaning back against the wall, but I couldn't think of anything to say. Whenever I tried my throat tightened.

April was like a porcupine, quills extended, daring someone to touch her. Whoever touched her went away with pain and scars. She had left all her friends and half her family in New Jersey. She seemed to be on a self-destruct mission, determined to destroy her new family. I stared at her face the same intense way she stared at it each morning in the mirror. Her lips were thin and almost colorless. She wouldn't pluck her eyebrows, so they were thicker than most girls', and your eyes went right to her eyes. They were gray, the color of New Jersey sky in the summertime when the pollution alerts were on. Strangely, she always wore her hair long and curly. It was a paradox: a romantic heap of curls surrounding a stony face. But when her face softened, it all fit together and she was quite appealing.

Behind that face is a little girl crying to be loved. I repeated that to myself. It was hard to believe.

I lay awake that night thinking about April. Her glare of hatred would not leave me.

I had tried to accept April, tried even to love her. I had covered for her with Dad and often taken her side in arguments. She never thanked me. She seemed to expect my good will, but when I gave it she would trample me.

She reminded me of a pet parakeet I once had. He loved to eat orange rinds. But if I opened the cage door and held out an orange rind to him, he would always attack my hand, pecking

furiously. I'd felt like grabbing him behind the neck and squeezing him between my fingers.

I only held back from lashing out at April for one reason: because she wanted me to attack her, to prove the world was weighted against her. She wanted my hatred, really. I wouldn't give it to her.

But neither could I give her love, at least in a way she would accept.

*I*t was a rough summer. In New Jersey, April had stayed out all night partying in Manhattan apartments. Here in New Mexico, she'd pick up some college guy and sleep under the cold desert sky, beside a river. Mother and Dad never knew when or even whether she'd return. Mother stopped talking about April to me so often, as if she had given up.

One night, when Mother and Dad were at a company banquet, I got a call from the Santa Fe police. They asked me to come down and identify a girl who claimed she was my sister. I trembled all the way there. When I saw the police station, I stepped on my brakes too sud-

HOUSEFUL OF STRANGERS

denly, and the tires screeched on the pavement.

April was in a room at the end of a long barred corridor. The concrete room was empty and the sound of our footsteps echoed off the walls as we entered. April was handcuffed to a metal stool in the center of the room. My stomach tightened. She looked like an animal just captured. Her hair was frazzled and sticking out from her head. Her T-shirt had been badly ripped, and the police had thrown a jacket over her to cover her. She looked at me, and her eyes seemed as gray as the dirty concrete walls. She wouldn't say it, but I knew she needed me.

The officer told me she and two guys had been spray-painting obscenities on some ancient Indian caves in a national park nearby. One of the guys was still being hunted in the hills, and the one they had caught claimed April hadn't done anything. If she were charged, it would be a federal offense.

I found myself explaining to the officer all about April's epilepsy and how the medicine sometimes affected her so that she lost control of herself. It was only partially true. He nodded, understanding. After a half-hour of questioning, I signed a release form for April. They had decided not to charge her.

During the drive home, my emotions ran between pity and anger. I couldn't push from my mind the image of April chained in a concrete cell. I couldn't forget her blank, expressionless stare. Wouldn't *anything* affect her? The angry side of me made me want to tell her off, to use this one chance to preach a sermon and show how she was wrecking her life. I had gone over the sermon mentally hundreds of times before. Every time April pulled one of her stunts, I went through it. And now, if ever, I had the right to deliver it. What could she say? She was at my mercy. She knew I could tell Dad about the arrest, and he just might ship her off to some reformatory.

The anger side and pity side fought until I pulled in the driveway. I reached over and touched her hand, and she didn't pull back. "April, why don't you take a bath and clean up some. I won't say anything."

I finally did get a chance for that sermon, after school started. April had taken the family car (against the rules; April wasn't supposed to drive alone because of her epilepsy) to buy some cigarettes. She must have had some kind of seizure, because she cracked up the car, breaking her pelvis and leg.

I visited her in the hospital every night. She wouldn't talk about the accident, but I think she felt embarrassed by it. To my parents' credit, they were cool. Their only concern was for April's comfort; they didn't bring up the matter of taking the car.

April's third night in the hospital, I was alone in the room with her. Her leg was in traction, which meant she had to lie flat on her back. She couldn't even see the television on the wall. She had lost weight, and without make-up she looked gaunt and pale. I stood beside her bed and read her some cards kids at school had sent with me.

"April, are you ever alone . . . completely alone, like you feel no one in the world understands?" I asked.

She looked at me sharply, then quickly looked away. "No."

"April, we love you, you know that, don't you? You're part of our family." The words almost stuck in my mouth. I had never told anyone in my family that I loved them. April knew it.

She hesitated a minute, then said, "Steve loves me, too." Steve was the guy who'd been caught at the Indian caves with her. She evaded me, but at least she didn't try to argue or strike back.

That's all I said. The rest of the sermon didn't seem to matter.

When Mother and Dad came, I had to go to the lobby—only two visitors were allowed in a room. There I thought about April and myself. What kept me from being like April? Why wasn't I the one who ran around vandalizing monuments, smashing cars, and cutting people down?

The waiting room was a good place to think. There was no laughter there, just small knots of people with worried looks on their faces, glancing at the clock. It was okay to be sad and reflective.

The difference between us, I decided, was that I had found a way to let go of things. I had learned to open up to God and to other people, even my parents. It was okay to admit wrong. There was such a thing as forgiveness.

April never had that option. She had built a prison around herself and nothing could escape. She couldn't forgive her mother for splitting up with her dad or her dad for leaving her. She couldn't forgive my father and me for stealing her mother's affection. She couldn't forgive herself for the thousand mean, stupid things she'd said to hurt us. It was all blocked up inside her, and she couldn't let it out.

Living with April had taught me one thing: love isn't like brute force. I kept wanting to reach inside her and change things. I wanted to remake her, fix up a few parts. But love seemed powerless, almost puny. Love hadn't done April any good in the past—what good would it do now? It just made me frustrated.

For a moment, I thought about how frustrating it must be for God (does God get frustrated?) as we refuse to respond to his love.

Who knows what will break through to April?

Could a boyfriend? A lover who really cared for her and forced her—no, that's the wrong word—helped her to open up?

Would it take a worse accident, one where she almost died and *had* to think about her life?

One last thought hit me like a stab of pain. What if April never opened up? What if her life ended, and she was still curled up, tightly clinging to herself, keeping God and the world out? She would have herself, all right, but that's all. God, that would be awful.

SURVIVAL
Verne Becker

I t strikes with no warning—the *problem.* And it's not a normal-sized one, either, one that you can work through with a week of worrying; rather, it's a colossal Problem with a capital P, the kind that makes you wonder whether you can cope for even another day. Wherever you turn, it's staring you in the face; whatever you do, it's there.

Take divorce, for instance—your parents' divorce. When they first break the news to you, you are shocked and upset. But soon you gather your wits together and try to distance yourself from your parents' troubles; "They've got their own lives to live and so do I," you say.

But it's never that simple. Their lives affect yours whether you want them to or not. You may have to move to a smaller house or apartment, and if so, you'll probably have to change schools. You may have to start coming home to an empty house after school. With two households for them to maintain, money will disappear quickly, leaving you with fewer dollars for new clothes. There may be only one car. And you may face the new experience of visiting one parent in his or her new home. You will see your mom and dad in a new way as they begin to date other people. Overhearing your name in their conversations with each other, you may feel like a commodity that must be supported, taken care of, and visited regularly. Sometimes your mom or dad

128

may get upset and irritable or explode in anger for no apparent reason.

Inevitably, these changes will stir up a lot of feelings in you; some you will be aware of, but others will remain hidden beneath the surface. Many people who go through their parents' divorce begin to hate themselves because they feel somehow responsible for the breakup. As a result, they can't concentrate on schoolwork, they daydream a lot, their grades go down. And the stress often leads to headaches or stomach aches. While one person may withdraw into a shell, another might get involved in a heavy relationship with a boyfriend or girlfriend, go to parties, and drink too much.

Not all of us face that situation, but sooner or later, we're all confronted with Problems. And when a Problem hits, your inner coping mechanisms spring into action. These mechanisms are common ways of dealing with such stressful circumstances as a death, divorce or separation in your family, physical or emotional abuse in your home, loss of a very close friend or relative, even moving to a new state. Any event that causes a major change in your normal living pattern can be stressful and can trigger your coping mechanisms. (A list of more mechanisms appears on pages 145–46.)

But how healthy are these mechanisms? Some of them, such as daydreaming, seem quite harmless; others, such as getting drunk or lashing out at people, can obviously cause physical or emotional damage. Just how healthy they are depends on the person and the circumstances, but all of them have something in common: They make it easier to *avoid* problems and stresses than to *face* them head on.

Coping mechanisms often take your mind off the real problem, either by putting your thoughts in neutral (alcohol, drugs, even too much radio or television) or by diverting them completely to other activities (exercise, overcommitment, fast living, sex). But if you allow the mechanisms to become substitutes for dealing with the problem directly, they can become, in turn, a bigger problem than the one you started with.

Consider two examples of how coping mechanisms work. Jason had a twenty-page term paper due in two weeks. Whenever he thought of doing research in the library, he would decide he was too busy and would put it off one more day. By the end of the first week, nothing had been done. Though he felt a great deal of pressure and tension as the second week began, he still found himself watching television one evening and going to Pizza Hut with friends on another. These activities helped him temporarily side-step the difficult task of researching and writing his paper.

Or consider Karen, who broke up with the guy she'd been dating for eight months. She was devastated; the constant companionship and security of those months were gone. A week after the breakup, a different guy asked her out. Immediately she latched on to him and allowed the relationship to become just as physical as the former one had been. It's quite possible that Karen unknowingly jumped into the new relationship to hide the rejection and hurt she felt over her "ex." Perhaps a few months of casual dating with no attachments would have given her time to recover from the breakup and learn some things about herself.

"Fearing the pain involved, almost all of us, to a greater or lesser degree, attempt to avoid problems," wrote psychiatrist Scott Peck in his book *The Road Less Traveled*. "We attempt to skirt around problems rather than meet them head on. We attempt to get out of them rather than suffer through them." The more serious the problem or source of stress, the greater your chances of avoiding the pain with desperate coping mechanisms such as drinking or drugs, severe depression, or outbursts of anger or violence.

Even an untrained eye can spot these mechanisms, particularly the extreme ones, in other people. We all know the guy who screeches down the street in his Trans Am after a fight with his girlfriend, or the attractive but insecure girl who starves herself for fear of gaining weight. The real challenge, however, is to learn to identify these mechanisms in ourselves. "It is in this whole process of meeting and solving problems that life has its meaning," Peck writes. "Problems are the cutting edge that distinguishes between success and failure. Problems call forth our courage and our wisdom; indeed, they create our courage and our wisdom. It is only because of problems that we grow mentally and spiritually."

These words come as a surprise to many. *Problems* give meaning to life? *Problems* help us grow? We usually expect the opposite to be true. Wouldn't the most enjoyable, meaningful life be problem-*free*—no struggles, no tough decisions, no pain? It sounds reasonable. But the simple fact is that no one—not even the richest or most famous person on earth—has a problem-free life. Everyone struggles with something. God chose not to remove all the problems of the world, not even for Christians; but instead, he decided to use those problems in our lives to help us get to know him, and ourselves, better. The more we face problems, the better we are able to grasp what God wants us to learn.

Many people in the Bible knew the importance of facing, rather than avoiding, the pain of problems. Think of Job. In the midst of his physical and emotional suffering, he searched himself for answers, questioned God, yet never gave up on him and learned much about man and God in the process. King David faced severe problems in his family and kingdom after his sin with Bathsheba, but rather than run away from his sin and the problems that followed, David admitted them, asked God's forgiveness, and moved ahead with God's blessing. Even Jesus, who did not want to endure the pain and suffering of the cross, set out for Jerusalem anyway. Later, as he prayed in the Garden of Gethsemane, he admitted to God his desire to avoid the cross if possible. But in spite of his feelings, he accepted God's will and went to his death. While most of our problems do not have consequences as weighty as those of Jesus and David, one principle is clear: We need to face, not avoid, our problems.

Where does God fit into this picture? How does he help us cope? Does he sweep into every difficult situation and apply a quick-fix, no-hassle solution? We have seen that he doesn't. His involvement is much deeper. He not only wants his people to conquer their problems, he also wants them to learn and grow. And he makes this growth process happen by asking us to *cooperate* with him in facing our problems.

The Bible refers to numerous situations in which God and man *worked together* to solve a problem. Jesus, for instance, must have had this in mind when he saw the blind man (John 9) and decided to heal him. All he had to do was say, "Be healed." But strangely, that's not what Jesus did. Instead, he spat in the dirt, stuck his fingers in it, and made mud. Then he smeared this mud on the man's eyes and told him to go wash off in the Pool of Siloam.

Why did Jesus do this? We're not told how the man felt at that moment, but he easily could have felt like the victim of a practical joke. If this man Jesus could heal people, then why didn't he just say the word and do it?

Jesus, however, wanted to do more than simply restore the man's eyesight. He wanted the man to *participate* in the healing. Jesus certainly had the power to do it alone, but he knew the man would benefit more from cooperation. Jesus, by wanting the man to participate, communicated this message: "I want you to trust me to do the best for you, and I want you to *take action* based on that trust. I want us to work together." Think about it: If the man hadn't acted and gone to wash, he might never have been healed.

The Apostle Paul also mentions this divine-human cooperation in Philippians 2:12b–13: "Continue to work out your salvation with fear and trembling, for it is God who works in you to will and to act according to his good pleasure" (NIV). Clearly,

God is in charge. But he entrusts us with the day-to-day working out of our lives. And as we work *out* those everyday problems— big and small—God works *in* us to bring about his will and to help us grow. That is what happened to most of the people who tell their stories in this book.

From these biblical passages and from the personal experiences you have read in these pages, two important principles stand out: First, God is ultimately in control of all that happens on Earth. No matter what the difficulty is, he has an even greater power to bring good from it. And second, God has given us the freedom and the responsibility to make choices and take action to cope with our problems. These two truths— God's power and our responsibility—stand side by side and are impossible to reconcile completely. But they are true nonetheless.

When we have a problem, God provides many ways of coping, but he leaves it up to us to choose which. That way we grow in the process of choosing, and we learn to exercise the awesome responsibility God has given us. Here are several kinds of help that God may provide:

—God may, and sometimes

does, intervene directly and supernaturally. He may miraculously heal an illness, protect someone from harm, or provide someone with a new job. God is able to do these things. But we shouldn't expect them; God tends to work in more ordinary ways.

—God may bring a special friend into your life who will be able to listen and empathize with your struggles. That person may not specialize in advice, but he or she can serve as a pressure valve and as someone who can support you, pray for you, and help you gain perspective. Your responsibility is to be aware of who those special friends might be, and then take the initiative to open yourself up to them and show them what you're going through.

—God may provide you with an especially helpful environment (church, youth group, home) that can give you love, encouragement, and support as you work through your problems. But again, you must show a willingness to risk talking about your problems. Most likely, you'll find others who will share their own struggles with you. This kind of environment enables you to both give and receive support.

—God may alert you to the need for professional help in dealing with your particular problem. Sometimes the effects of crises such as a death in the family, a divorce, physical or mental abuse in your family, rape or some other sexual trauma, or other life-shattering crises can be so great that a trained, professional counselor is needed to aid in the healing process. But if that is the case, you need to take the first step in asking your pastor or youth director to refer you to a professional in your area.

—God can give you comfort and security as you read the Bible and trust him for support and guidance. "I waited patiently for God to help me; then he listened and heard my cry," the psalmist wrote. "He lifted me out of the pit of despair, out from the bog and the mire, and set my feet on a hard, firm path and steadied me as I walked along" (40:1–2). You'll find words of hope and support throughout Scripture; the Psalms are an especially good place to start. For a sampling, look at Psalms 27, 32, 34, 40, 46, and 112.

A re you struggling with a Problem right now? Are

you finding some aspect of student or family life to be almost unbearable? Are you wondering whether you'll survive? Whatever your Problem is—loneliness, failure, family tensions, bad habits—the message of this book, and the message of the Bible, is that you *can* cope. You *will* survive. Psalm 34:19 says, "The good man does not escape all troubles—he has them too. But the Lord helps him in each and every one." No one's life is free from problems. Everyone has them, even Christians. God never promises that your problems will go away; but he does promise his presence and help. You can trust him for that.

The writer of Psalm 112 describes the results when a person trusts in God: "Such a man will not be overthrown by evil circumstances. . . . He does not fear bad news, nor live in dread of what may happen. For he is settled in his mind that Jehovah will take care of him. That is why he is not afraid, but can calmly face his foes" (112:6–8). With this kind of trust in God, you can develop the ability to face your problems and work toward solving them.

Coping with difficult situations and personal problems requires two things: trusting God and taking responsibility. Both are necessary. Trusting God and sitting around waiting for him to take care of everything won't get you anywhere. Nor will trying to do everything on your own, with no regard for God's wishes. But if you learn to balance these two attitudes you will go a long way toward solving your problems. And you will grow as a person in the process.

PERSONAL STRESS TEST

Below are some of the ways we respond to stress and some of the results. They are grouped into four categories, corresponding to the four major "areas" of our lives. See how many of these coping mechanisms you've experienced at some point in your life. And if you're experiencing any of these on a regular basis, consider following some of the suggestions given on the previous pages.

Responses and/or Results

Physical

Throw yourself into sports and exercise
Overeat or undereat
Smoke cigarettes, drink alcohol, use drugs
Overload your schedule
Have trouble sleeping; sleep too much
Get sick easily
Develop chronic disorders such as ulcers, headaches, or rashes

Mental/Emotional

Worry a lot
Hold your feelings inside
Lash out at people, sometimes for little or no apparent reason
Daydream frequently
Procrastinate
Have difficulty concentrating on schoolwork
Find little enjoyment in life
Have sustained periods of unexplained depression
Rationalize or intellectualize your feelings; minimize the problem
Exaggerate the problem, side-stepping the real issue
Blame the problem on everyone else
Blame yourself, condemn yourself, or feel sorry for yourself
Ignore or deny your feelings and concentrate only on facts
Immerse your mind in "filler" activities such as television, music, video or fantasy games, or reading
Deny that you have a problem, even if others call it to your attention

Social

Live in the "fast lane"—fill all your time with people, activity, entertainment, etc.

Hide your struggles from people by maintaining an "up" image

Become physically and/or emotionally involved with a boyfriend or girlfriend

Use other people to meet your needs

Allow others to make decisions for you about your behavior or attitudes.

Withdraw from people physically and emotionally

Spiritual

Set aside your feelings and praise God anyway

Do nothing, assuming God will work things out

Blame God for what happened

Doubt whether God is real or whether he is truly good

Discard your faith as meaningless and useless

Attribute your problem to someone else's sin

Blame the problem on your own sin, but try unsuccessfully to solve the problem or change

Assume that every single thing that happens to you is God's will

Immerse yourself in numerous "spiritual" activities such as church-going, Bible studies, Campus Life/Young Life, your church youth group, even service projects for other people